A Very Byzantine Journey

Discovering the New Testament Story through Icons and Pilgrimage

— J. RICHARD SMITH —

Sacristy Press

Sacristy Press
PO Box 612, Durham, DH1 9HT

www.sacristy.co.uk

First published in 2022 by Sacristy Press, Durham

Sacristy Limited, registered in England & Wales, number 7565667

British Library Cataloguing-in-Publication Data
A catalogue record for the book is available from the British Library

ISBN 978-1-78959-216-0

This book is dedicated to a small group of people.

First to my parents, Diana and the late Irvine Smith, and to my sister Alison Smith.

Also, to my three "priest friends", Fathers Gary Bradley, Anthony Speakman and Andrew Wakeham-Dawson.

My four children, Cameron, Victoria, Madeleine and Lara, who provide a bedrock for all these adventures and have been with Dad through thick and thin.

Two couples, Professor Al Richardson and his wife Andrea and Professor Hani Gabra and his wife Diana, have all four contributed to this book more than they can guess.

My parents moulded me, and my three "priest friends" have introduced me to a whole new world in what I sincerely hope is my midlife. Horizons have opened for me which I could never have dreamt of, but for their influence. My children give me great joy (mostly)! Alison, Al, Andrea, Hani and Diana—thank you. My sincerest thanks to all.

Contents

Illustrations

Foreword

Richard has written an inspirational sequel to his previous book, *The Journey: Spirituality, Pilgrimage, Chant.*

This book incorporates pilgrimage, travelogue and the New Testament story, as told in Eastern Orthodox iconography, with visits to those sites today.

Richard writes in a highly readable, engaging style with personal accounts of his journeys, meetings with people on the way and graphic descriptions of the fascinating places he has visited. He includes comments which range from the poignant to the humorous in ways which make his "travelogue" so "human" that it is hard to put the book down!

He follows the origin of the original iconographic image of Christ, "not made by human hands", which proved to be the progenitor of all subsequent images of Christ. This image may well have been the original face cloth from Christ's tomb. He also seeks to explain the esoteric meaning of icons and their ability to show the "something other" of great spiritual significance hidden behind the icon.

Richard summarizes the significance of his message: "If you are a person who wants to see where history was made, you can visit the sites of the events portrayed in the icons... Icons themselves are not the dull art form perceived in the West but tell the really important parts of the New Testament story. They are a perfect adjunct to contemplative prayer and there is much hidden allegory which is interpretable once you know the genre" (page 113).

Richard takes us on those journeys, combining entertaining accounts of his travels to these sites with profound interpretations of their spiritual symbolism.

As a person who had not previously understood the inspirational nature of icons, I will always be grateful to Richard for opening my spiritual eyes to their true meaning.

The Baroness Cox
September 2021

Acknowledgements

I have been very fortunate to have been supported in this interest by my three friends who are priests and advisors: Father Gary Bradley and Father Anthony Speakman, Vicar and erstwhile Curate respectively of the Parish of Little Venice, London; and Group Captain, the Rev Dr Andrew Wakeham-Dawson, Chaplain to the RAF. I also have been wonderfully encouraged by the late Mrs Maria Andipa of the Andipa Gallery, London, also Chairman of the Ionian Society of London. Maria has helped me obtain icons at great personal effort to her and mercifully low cost to me! I also owe a debt of gratitude to Sir Richard Temple, a gentleman and scholar of icons and things monastic, both Christian and Buddhist. I have learned much from his writings and have quoted from his book *Icons and the Mystical Origins of Christianity*. I am grateful for his insights.

I am very grateful to Natalie Watson, Publishing Director at Sacristy Press, for her editorial suggestions, which much improved my original manuscript. All that is written is mine; however, some reordering and deletions improved things greatly.

I am also indebted once again to Petroula and Kostos Stergiou, the proprietors of the Petra Hotel, Grikos on Patmos, for their wonderful hospitality and generosity in welcoming me back to the island and for providing such a wonderful and inspiring writing venue. In addition, I am so grateful to Yiorgos, Gerty and Christina Moraiti and to Christina's husband Tassos Koutsouvelis and their son Vasilios for their kindness, hospitality and a wonderful writing space on Ithaka.

I would also like to thank my two younger children, Madeleine and Lara, for allowing me undisturbed writing time. My two older children, Cameron and Victoria, are now beyond university, and my travels thus have much less impact on them these days. Also, thanks are due to Catrina Donegan for her editorial help and with family matters when I was away. My sister Alison and mother Diana also deserve my thanks for all their support. Alison proofread the final document and made some essential deletions. Mr Ben Jones, my research fellow, has given much IT support, and Ms Rodena Kelman has helped me with her superb organization. My daughter Madeleine made a late but invaluable contribution at the picture importation stage and in picture editing. Her younger sister, Lara, has also been supportive with IT issues at which I am poor; Lara also has a keen sense of religiosity and much mischief! Finally, as this book has gone through various drafts, I would like to thank Sara Bedford and John Harrison for both encouragement and much-valued criticism; without both there would be no book. The version you are reading is of course entirely my responsibility, "warts and all".

The author

My name is Richard Smith, and I was born in Falkirk in Scotland. I was educated at Dollar Academy and thereafter at Glasgow University where I qualified with a medical degree in 1982. After this, I undertook a thesis on the interaction of viruses and cervical cancer, graduating with an MD from Glasgow University. I am a Fellow of the Royal College of Obstetricians and Gynaecologists, and for the last thirty years I have lived and worked in London with the exception of a brief sabbatical in New York. I currently work as a gynaecological surgeon at Imperial College, London, based at Hammersmith, Queen Charlotte's and Charing Cross Hospitals, and also the Lister Hospital, Chelsea, London.

The photographer

All the icons have been photographed by Ashley Straw. Ashley has been working as a professional photographer for over twenty-five years. He started out in photojournalism, working for several London-based press agencies, specializing in portraiture and documentary commissions. Over the years he has expanded into automotive, product and architectural commissions, even photographing the occasional wedding.

The travelling companions

There are a number of travelling companions mentioned in this book. The first is the Revd Dr Andrew Wakeham-Dawson, priest, scientist, entomologist and all-round good guy. Whatever disaster unfolds, Andrew is never fazed, which makes one feel safe, particularly when travelling in places with some element of natural or urban risk. There is my former wife Deborah Boyle, and then there are three friends: Xiaomei Mi, and Hani and Diana Gabra. Xiaomei is a doctor of Chinese medicine and a businesswoman. Hani is Professor of Medical Oncology at Imperial College and his wife Diana is a broadcaster and professional pianist. We have had trips to Lebanon and Cairo, both quite remarkable and revelatory. Without the Gabra influence, I suspect I would never have been brave enough to visit some of the places we did. We had much fun. Finally, I also had the great joy to visit Mystras in the Peloponnese with Dr Angeliki Rouvali, another wonderfully erudite friend.

Introduction

There is a myriad of books available on the history of icons, their meaning, and their place within the Orthodox Church. I have many of them in my bookcase. There are also some which tell you how to pray with icons, but there is not a practical guide as to how they illustrate the Christian story and how, with understanding, they can deepen faith.

There are many iconographic themes based on apocryphal gospels. With one exception, I have not used these images, but stuck to the original idea, namely to tell the New Testament story as it is told, following more or less the order of St Luke's Gospel. I cannot help but love the fact that Luke, as opposed to the other Gospel writers, tells the story in a semblance of chronological order. St Luke was a physician writing for a non-Jewish audience, and he knew what they wanted! As a fellow physician, I can relate to this.

I am very fortunate to have visited many of the places where the New Testament story happened and to place the iconographic themes derived from it into a genuine geographical context. We live in an era where many of the Gospel stories are seen as just that, stories. If, however, you visit these places the historicity becomes much clearer and, at least to me, much more real—I'm afraid I am a bit of a "doubting Thomas". As a scientist, it's hard not to be, and I respect Thomas for his desire to put his hand "in the hole" in Christ's side. This book therefore seeks to trace the New Testament story through travelogue; hence the photos showing places as they are now and as they are linked to iconography.

There is also a paucity of writing on the origins of icons and how the images have been passed down. The image of Christ is always portrayed in a similar way, classically with long hair parted with a little central tuft of hair. Where did this image come from? Almost certainly the starting point is the Cloth of Edessa, about which I will have more to say later. I have chased this image and its history from Constantinople (Istanbul),

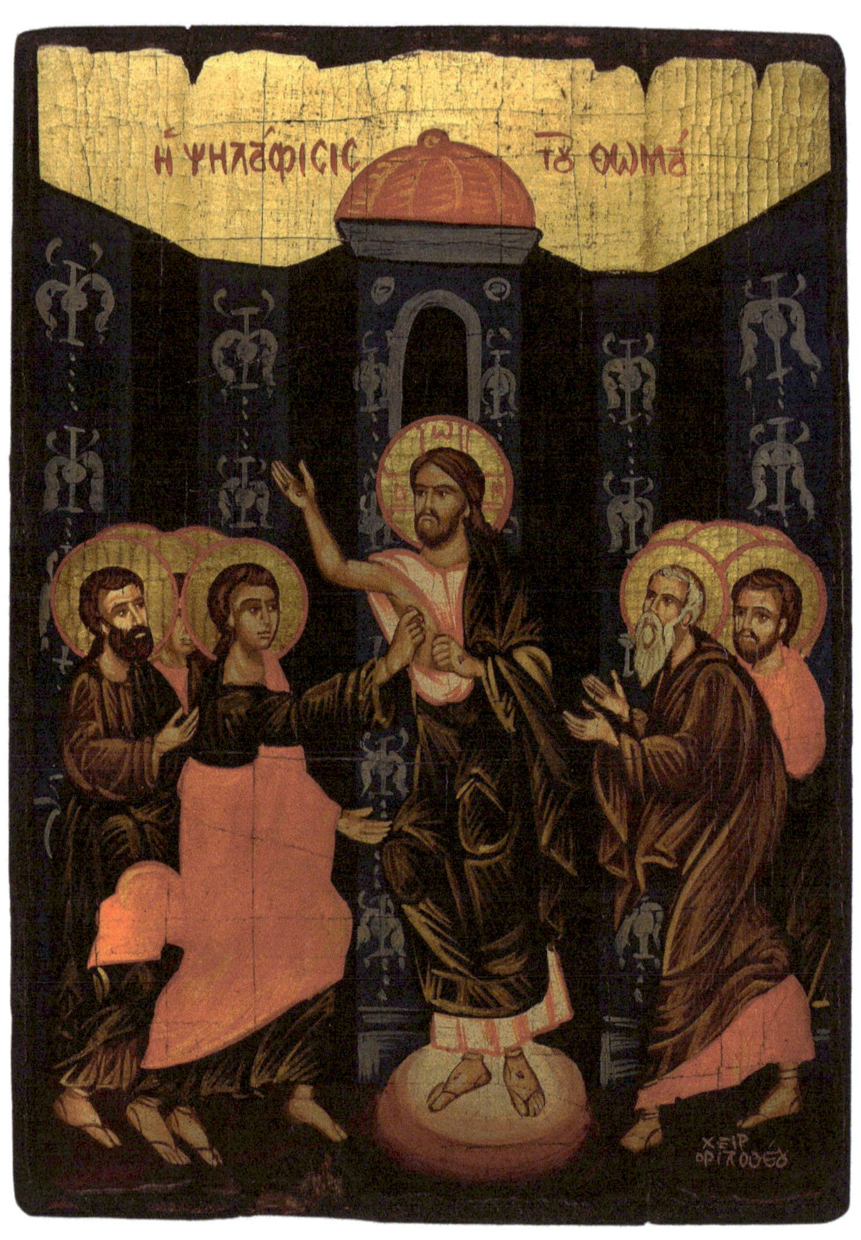

St Thomas and the Risen Christ

to Rome, to its current "hiding place" in a basilica high in the hills of the Majella National Park. Its authenticity is likely and its significance great.

Icons are embedded in Orthodoxy, so much so that the Feast of Orthodoxy celebrates the Byzantine Emperor Michael III and his mother, the Empress Theodora, who restored icons to religious life in AD 843. (For the record, Michael III was a pleasure-loving ruler, known later as Michael the Drunkard by his successor's chroniclers, in an attempt to besmirch his reputation; he sounds like quite a good fellow to me!) Returning to icons, after a century of strife, when they were banned and destroyed, they again became a central part of worship. This was akin to the Reformation in Scotland, where John Knox preached against religious idolatry and all visual images were destroyed; the reverse process is perhaps just awakening!

Almost all of the icons pictured in this book are owned by me. This may give the impression that I must be wealthy; far from it. If you have holidayed in Greece, you will have seen many of these icons in souvenir shops. It is one of the best things about icons; there is no such thing as plagiarism. All images can be copied and many of the images in the book were very cheap (by way of cost, not content). They are, however, true to the tradition.

The idea to write the book came about on a summer holiday. I was with my family on the island of Ithaki, the home of Odysseus, in Greece. I took my sister into the church in the village of Kioni and explained the iconostasis to her icon by icon. First, she was stunned by the beauty of the church, but she also much appreciated her new-found understanding of the story portrayed by the icons. Both of us were brought up in the Presbyterian Church of Scotland. I am an Anglo-Catholic with a deep interest in Orthodoxy. Alison married, and later was divorced from, a good man who is Roman Catholic, and she brought her children up in this faith. We have both therefore deviated a long way from our upbringing. Our mother was brought up as a Methodist, moved to Anglicanism as a boarding school pupil at Lincoln High School for Girls near the Cathedral, and for some time was an Elder in the Church of Scotland. She is a latter-day fan of icons and things Orthodox.

Most Orthodox homes have an icon corner, the rich ones a private chapel. There is an ever-increasing interest in this subject and most

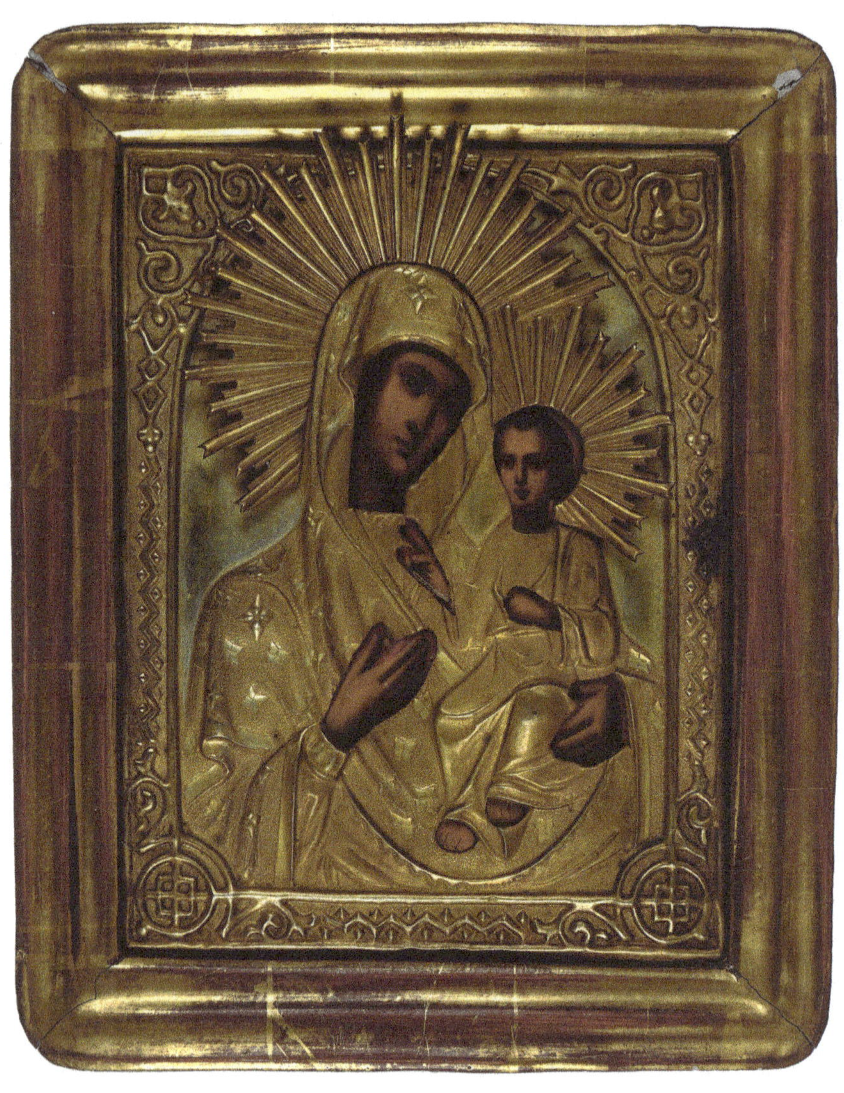

The Virgin and Child, the Tikhvinskaya

Anglican churches and cathedrals now have icons on display, usually of the Virgin and Child, and Christ Pantocrator (see pages 4 and 7). The meaning of these is obvious, although there is almost always more to be discovered.

I am also keen to explore the hidden imagery of icons. Perhaps the reason there are no books laid out in the New Testament order is precisely because the greater understanding one develops, the less important is the order in which the story is told. They all stand alone, telling their own individual story. Much of this relates to gnosis—a knowledge of spiritual mysteries—and is also linked to the practice of repetitive prayer. Icons are vehicles which help us to understand the mystical aspect of Christianity, and when coupled with repetitive prayer allow access to the inner self. This practice is also found in the world's other great contemplative religions. This book is of a Christian nature, because that is what I understand and practise, but there is much synergy with other religions, particularly Buddhism, Hinduism, Sufi Muslim and certain Jewish sects.

The image on page 4 is Russian and is entitled the Tikhvinskaya; it is an icon of the Virgin of Tikhvin. On the back, in faded writing, it says it was brought from Russia to England in the 1870s by J. M. Bazin. It is a Russian middle-class travelling icon, set in a wooden frame with an opening glass door. The tradition is that the icon of the Virgin of Tikhvin was transported miraculously by angels from Constantinople in 1383. It appeared above the waters of Lake Ladoga, and it then came to rest in the town of Tikhvin in the land of Novgorod. Over the centuries many miracles were attributed to it.

Pantocrator means Ruler of All. The original version of this icon dates from the sixth century and is situated in St Catherine's Monastery on Mount Sinai. To quote Sir Richard Temple:

> From Greek Antiquity comes the type of the bearded philosopher-teacher with the two fingers of the right hand raised in the "teaching" gesture. From the same period comes the book, signifying knowledge and wisdom. The voluminous cloak or himation was the traditional garb of the philosophers while its purple colour indicates royalty. Above in the background, in a

> Pythagorean or neo-Platonic allusion to cosmic powers is the solar disc or halo, a form that can be traced back to ancient Egypt, while the two stars may have astrological connotations associated with Zoroastrian magic.
>
> We are brought to the threshold of the meaning of existence. This is why traditionally, in icons of Christ, the nimbus around the head contains letters signifying the mystery of Existence: *Ho on* (w ON), meaning "Existence", The Being, or "I am that I am" as the Authorized version has it. The sense is similar to "That Which Is 'of the Brahmins and is related to the *path of self-knowledge* of Hindu mysticism and to the Socratic' *know thyself*".*

The version seen on page 7 needs no further explanation except to add that it is a nineteenth-century Russian aristocratic travelling icon. It is boxed in ebony, surrounded by gold leaf and the Oklad is silver. The image is the same, as is the meaning!

---

* R. Temple, *Icons and the Mystical Origins of Christianity* (London: Element, 1990), pp. 92–3. Kind permission to use this quote from Sir Richard Temple.

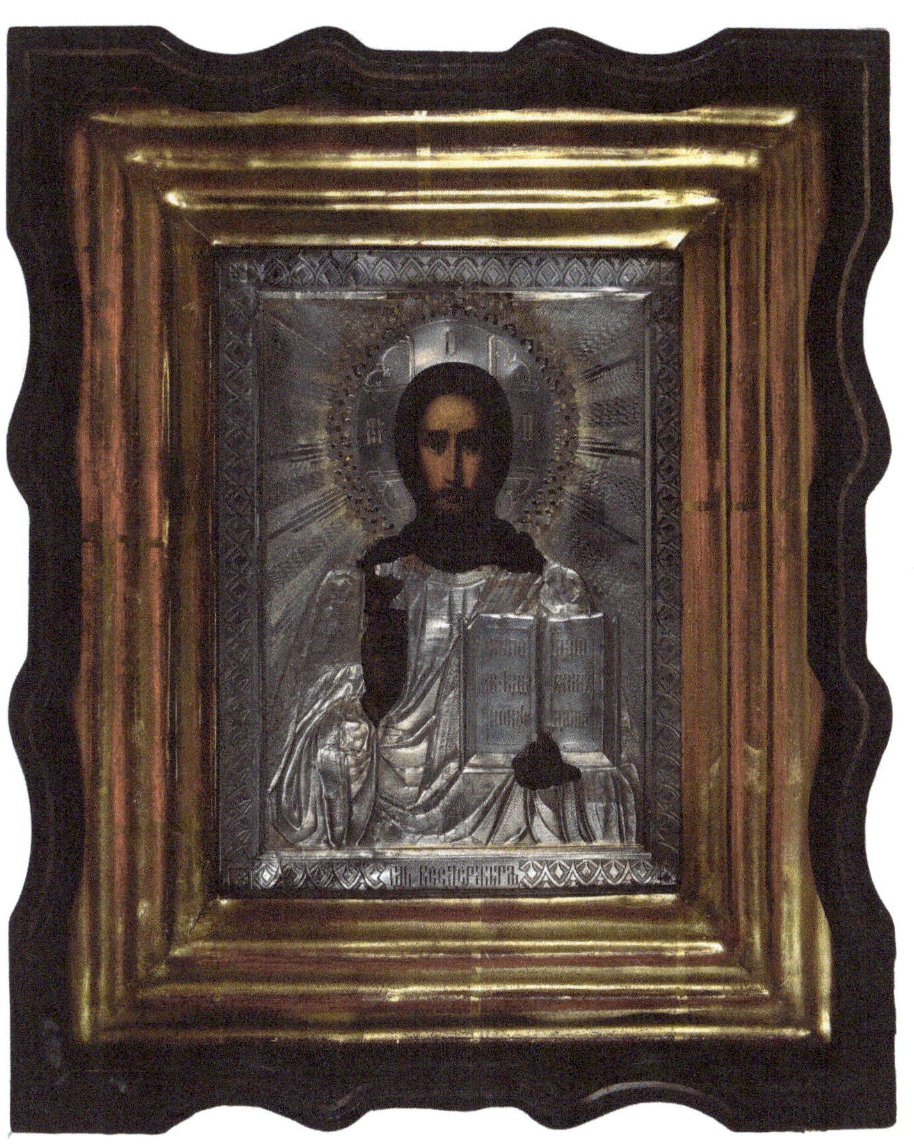

Christ Pantocrator

1

Iconographic art: its history and inner meaning

Icons have long been a much-disparaged art form, frequently maligned by art critics in the West. Orthodox religious art has been considered somehow inferior to what had developed in the West. The comparison is always made with Renaissance art, particularly Italian altar pieces. At first sight, the Eastern Orthodox versions of the various themes seem primitive at best. This is, however, to misunderstand the meaning behind the icons, literally. Why I say "literally, behind" is that they all deliberately have reverse perspective, the reason for which is that the true message is not in the picture but behind it. Most religions decry the use of imagery in search of the holy. In Islam, there are no images of the Prophet, in Judaism there is no image of Yahweh, and in the Presbyterian Church likewise there are no images; the message is in the word. Much of this originates with the turmoil which followed from Israelites' worship of the Golden Calf.

Of course, music and singing are appropriate in all the traditions: the rich contribution of Bach I will touch on later.

Byzantine art tried to solve this conundrum by adopting reverse perspective so that the image itself was not important, but what lay behind the image. There also was a tradition that all iconographic images could be copied since they were religious rather than commercial, and the artist never signed the piece. Traditionally icons are painted by monks, who work prayerfully to create the images.

There is also the concept, which we will explore later, of the image "not made by human hands". One can only speculate, but the Cloth of Edessa and the Shroud of Turin must have been perceived as being of inestimable value to the early Christians. However, death cloths are ritually unclean to Jewish people, and one must remember that all the disciples, Jesus' original followers and Jesus himself were Jewish. This must have created great difficulties for those early Christians and probably would have led to great secrecy surrounding the cloths.

The Catholic Church has tried to distance itself from the conjecture that continues over the Cloth of Edessa. Pope Benedict XVI, a man of discernment and a great theologian, declared it to be authentic as far as he was concerned.

Renaissance art was regarded as devotional and became progressively more beautiful, which of course led to greater appreciation of the art over the message. It played a small part in the causes of the Reformation, and although it was only small, when the Reformation came many images were destroyed. Ironically, by its simplicity, iconographic art has continued to thrive until modern times. If you are ever in doubt about the artistic talents of the earlier painters, you only need to look at the work of the Cretan artist El Greco, who painted both icons and "normal" art for the King of Spain. Also, Andrei Rublev, whilst strictly iconographic, demonstrated enormous sensitivity in the subjects he painted.

Most of ancient Western art is centred around religion, which I know drove my somewhat atheistic daughter Victoria mad on her History of Art degree course. "Too much Jesus, Dad!" What did she expect?

It is difficult to know when icon painting first started, but St Luke is attributed as the earliest iconographer. I have seen an icon attributed to him that resides in a side chapel in the monastery of Iviron, on Mount Athos. It is of course impossible to know whether it really was painted by St Luke, but it demonstrates that the iconographic tradition probably dates from the very earliest days of Christianity. The fact that these two cloths—the Cloth of Edessa and the Shroud of Turin—lay, well-guarded and secret, in the Chapel of the Imperial Byzantine Emperor's palace, would also go some way to explain the Byzantine love of the medium. This lasted until the first iconoclasm between AD 726 and 787; the second iconoclasm was between 814 and 842. At both times, the Emperors Leo III and Leo V declared that all icons were in effect graven images and should be destroyed. As always with this type of religious edict feelings ran very high and much blood was shed. Most icons before this date were destroyed, only a few surviving in out-of-the-way places, such as the monastery of St Catherine in Sinai, where there are many. It is thought that the number of icons preceding this date can be counted in tens.

I had the great privilege many years ago to meet Fr Vito Borgia, at the time in his late eighties. My then-wife Deborah and I were on holiday in Malta with the family and had decided that the two of us, without the children, would visit the Cathedral of St John in Valetta. We had worried that the children might be too noisy, but on entering the very splendid and beautiful cathedral there was unfortunately a terrible racket from the thousands of tourists, even in the areas where silence was demanded. It felt as if God had gone out for the afternoon! We left the cathedral after looking round and wandered around the corner to find the church, Our Lady of Damascus. This was a beautiful little church built in the Greek tradition with an iconostasis of many icons, including a particularly beautiful one behind the altar. We returned to our hotel, but I was keen to go back to, slightly naughtily, take some photos at a later date.

Sure enough, the opportunity arose a few days later when we were all in Valetta, and Madeleine, at the time a baby, was in a backpack on my back. I arrived at the church, but to get my camera out of the backpack, I had to take it off, always a delicate manoeuvre, then hoist pack and child back on to my back. As I did this, I noticed an elderly priest looking down on me from a first-floor window. I entered the church and was about to take a photo when I heard the noise of footsteps to the side of the altar and the priest appeared though a side door. I quickly pocketed my camera without being caught or for that matter taking any photos. The priest was absolutely charming and introduced himself, and then gave me and my baby daughter a guided tour of his church. He blessed both Madeleine and me and allowed us behind the iconostasis to see the icon more closely. I said to him, "Surely we are not allowed behind the iconostasis?" In Greece, no women or children were allowed such access; it was usually limited to the clergy. This was when he pointed out that he was Roman Catholic but practising the Greek rites, since his church predated the Schism between Orthodoxy and Roman Catholicism. His icon had been brought to Malta from Damascus to save it from destruction and thus predated the iconoclasm. In AD 843, the situation was reversed by the Emperor Michael III and his mother, the Empress Theodora, who changed the Edict. Icons were restored.

The iconographic tradition continued in the territories of the Byzantine Empire. After the adoption of Orthodoxy by the Russians, the tradition also flowered there and across all the Slavic lands. In the Holy Republic of Mount Athos, all the Orthodox countries have their monasteries, or sketes. I have stayed at the Romanian skete of Prodromou (John the Baptist) and visited the Russian monastery of St Panteleimon, as well as many of the Greek monasteries.

The tradition is certainly very much alive and thriving today across the traditional Orthodox world but also in the UK and USA. Aidan Hart is probably the UK's foremost icon painter, and he is passing this tradition on via his books and classes. HRH, The Prince of Wales has also been a big supporter of these classes, which help to spread the tradition.

Rublev's Trinity shows the angels representing the Trinity of Father, Son and Holy Ghost as they appeared to Abraham and his wife Sarah at the oaks of Mamre (Genesis 18:1–15). Although poor, they prepared a feast for the travellers, not realizing who they were. And despite their old age, they became parents of a son.

Hesychastic monks were and are practised in inner prayer. This is well described in the book *The Philokalia*, a collection of texts written by the hesychastic practitioners of the Eastern Orthodox Church. The *Philokalia* was translated into English by Philip Sherrard and Metropolitan Kallistos Ware between 1979 and 1995. There is a single-volume, shortened version of the *Philokalia*, which makes for an excellent basic understanding; the level I am at, at very best.

An excellent introduction to hesychasm is also found in a book of unknown authorship, *The Way of a Pilgrim*, which, some have speculated, may have been written by Tolstoy. In it, an unfortunate man who is disabled, then widowed, then rendered homeless by his brother, becomes a wanderer. He is desperate to learn how to pray. Eventually on his travels he meets a monk, a Starets, who becomes his spiritual teacher, and he suggests that he follow St Paul's instruction, namely "to pray without ceasing". He is taught the Jesus Prayer or The Prayer of the Heart, the repetition of "Lord Jesus Christ, have mercy on me, a sinner". By learning how to pray in this way, as well as being part of regular religious life, the

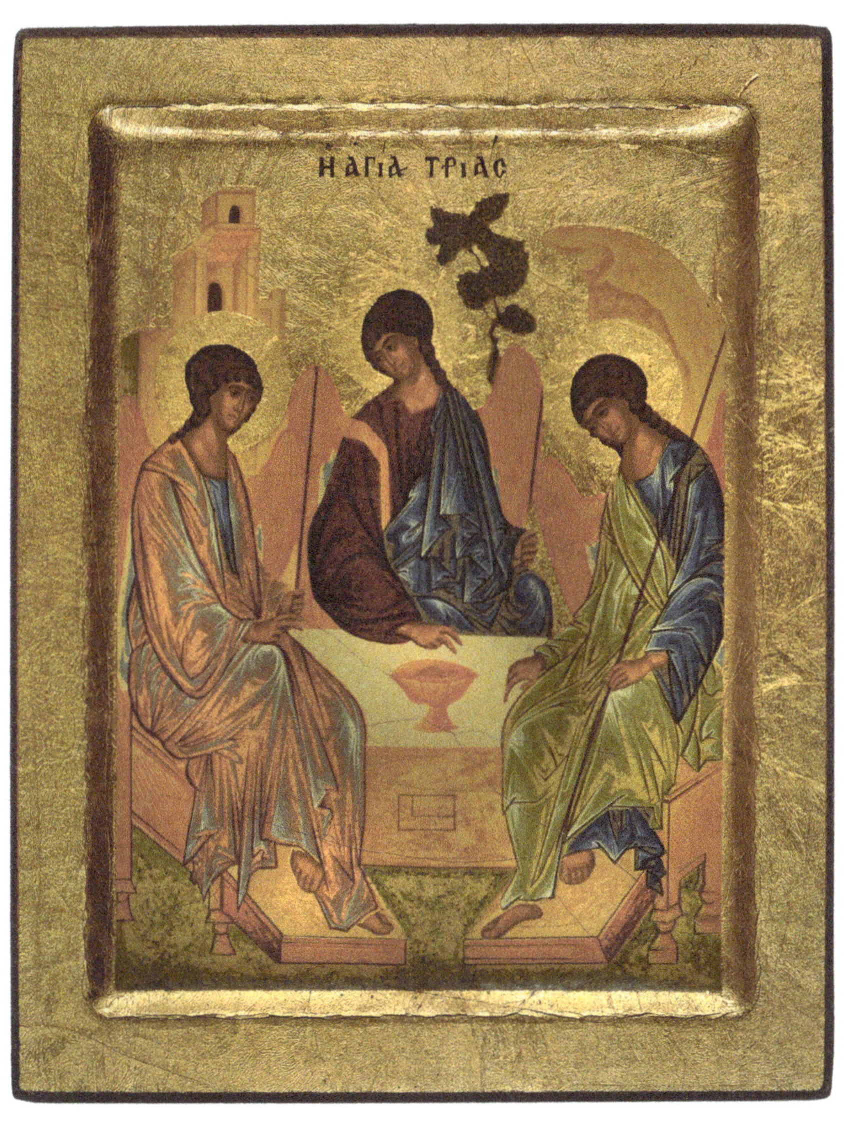

The Rublev Icon of the Trinity

wanderer discovers inner peace and the ability to avoid daily distractions from his spiritual life.

By understanding the mystical Christian route to inner silence, one then understands how the monks who created the iconographic images sought to represent the spiritual rather than the physical. The spiritual life has been compared to stepping into another room which you have not seen before: finding the kingdom of God in such a way is the pearl beyond price.

The iconographic image originated in the Graeco-Roman tradition, but we know that the original portraits which resemble icons are known as Fayum portraits. These were produced in the Egyptian desert at the Fayum oasis, where it is thought an Essene community existed. Jesus himself was thought to be part of the Essene community based above the Dead Sea at Qumran.

In the same tradition, the Church Fathers also settled in the Egyptian desert, following the example of St Anthony, who sought complete solitude in prayer. From these early monastic foundations, it is likely that what became Celtic Christianity was exported from Egypt to Ireland, and thence to Scotland, then down through Lindisfarne and northern England, moving further south with St Chad in Lastingham and Lichfield and then across the Channel to Europe.

It is therefore likely that these exquisitely peaceful images resulted from an amalgam of these ideas. However, the Hellenic Platonic ideas of hierarchy within the spiritual world were also brought into play. As you can see on the diagrams on page 15, the clear correlation of Platonic cosmology and its later Christian version are striking. Like Platonism, Christianity sees the world on different levels: the Divine, the Hand of God, Light, Angels, Christ/Virgin Mary/Saints, Man, The Ground (Earth), The lower world, and finally the Kingdom of Darkness (cave).

There is a small crescent at the top of the image which represents the Divine; if you mentally continue the crescent to make an invisible circle, it is much larger than the whole picture. The Hand of God is then visible, delivering celestial light. The angels sit at this level, below which is the enthroned Christ, the Virgin Mary and the Saints.

Below these is Man and he rests upon the Ground. (Christ, the Virgin and Saints never have their feet on the ground.) The ground is

Scheme showing the three stages of man in the universe according to Plato

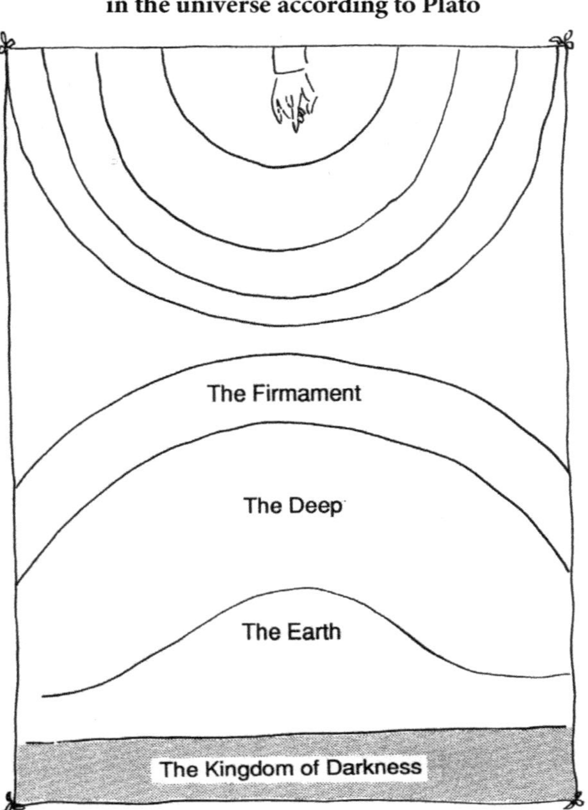

Diagram of the universe according to Christian cosmology

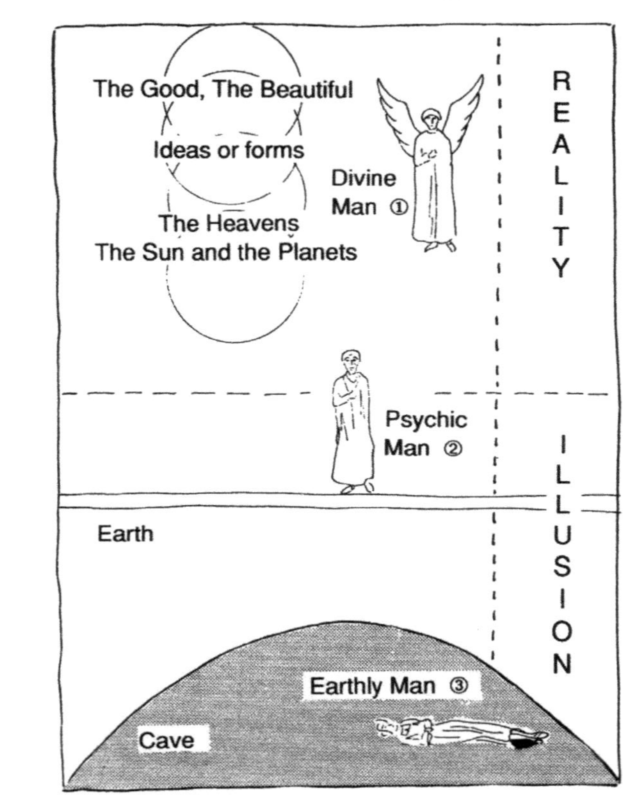

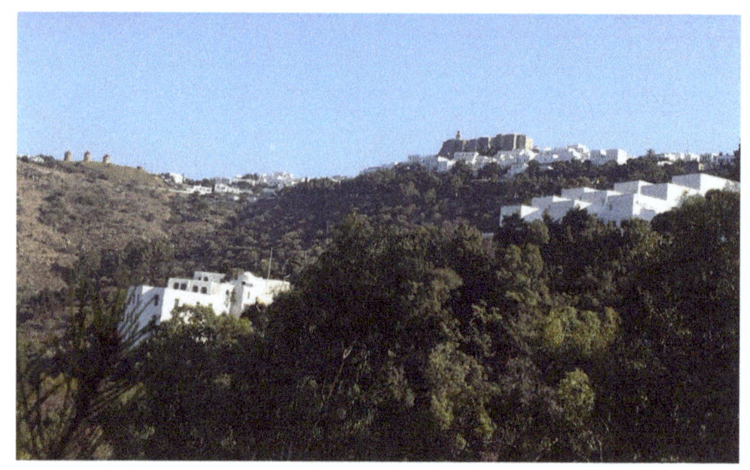

Patmos showing the Cave of the Apocalypse and the Monastery of St John the Divine on the horizon

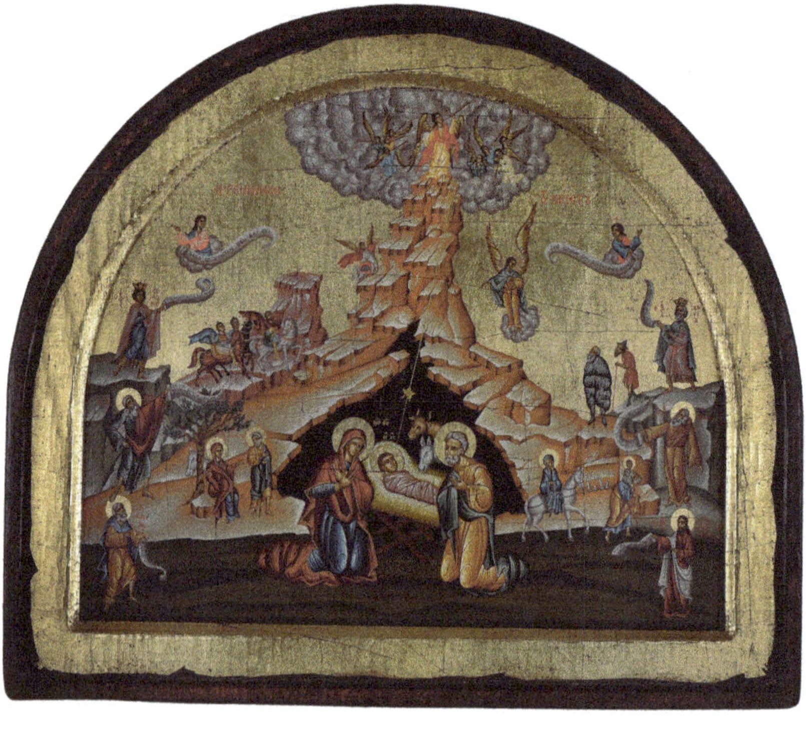

The Nativity of Christ

where unspiritually developed man resides; then below all of this is the Kingdom of Darkness.

The cave is a common theme: Christ was born in a cave; St John had his revelation in a cave.

In all icons, angels always look up to the Divine; Christ, the Virgin and the Saints are looking at us with great inner peace, and men are usually represented as involved in spiritual struggle. The Earth is represented by a rocky landscape and the Cave is the place of spiritual darkness.

Of course, part of the cleverness is that there is always a dual hidden message. The icon shows an image of the physical world and that is all that most people see; however, underlying this is the spiritual message of the image, the original of which was created by Christian spiritual masters who understood spiritual warfare because they had experienced it themselves. No aspect of the icon is ever down to chance! Once, however, you understand the idiom, the genre makes complete sense, at least most of the time. For those interested in exploring these matters in much greater depth I would commend to you Dick Temple's erudite and excellent book, from which I have quoted, *Icons and the Mystical Origins of Christianity.*

The icon on page 18 depicts St John in the Cave of the Apocolypse in the Isle of Patmos. He is dictating the book of Revelation to his disciple St Prochorus, and John is listening to the voice of heaven.

Revelation 21:1–6

> And I saw a new heaven and a new earth: for the first heaven and the first earth were passed away; and there was no more sea.
>
> And I John saw the holy city, new Jerusalem, coming down from God out of heaven, prepared as a bride adorned for her husband.
>
> And I heard a great voice out of heaven saying, Behold, the tabernacle of God is with men, and he will dwell with them, and they shall be his people, and God himself shall be with them, and be their God.

And God shall wipe away all tears from their eyes; and there shall be no more death, neither sorrow, nor crying, neither shall there be any more pain: for the former things are passed away.

And he that sat upon the throne said, Behold, I make all things new. And he said unto me, Write: for these words are true and faithful.

And he said unto me, It is done. I am the Alpha and the Omega, the beginning and the end. I will give unto him that is athirst of the fountain of the water of life freely.

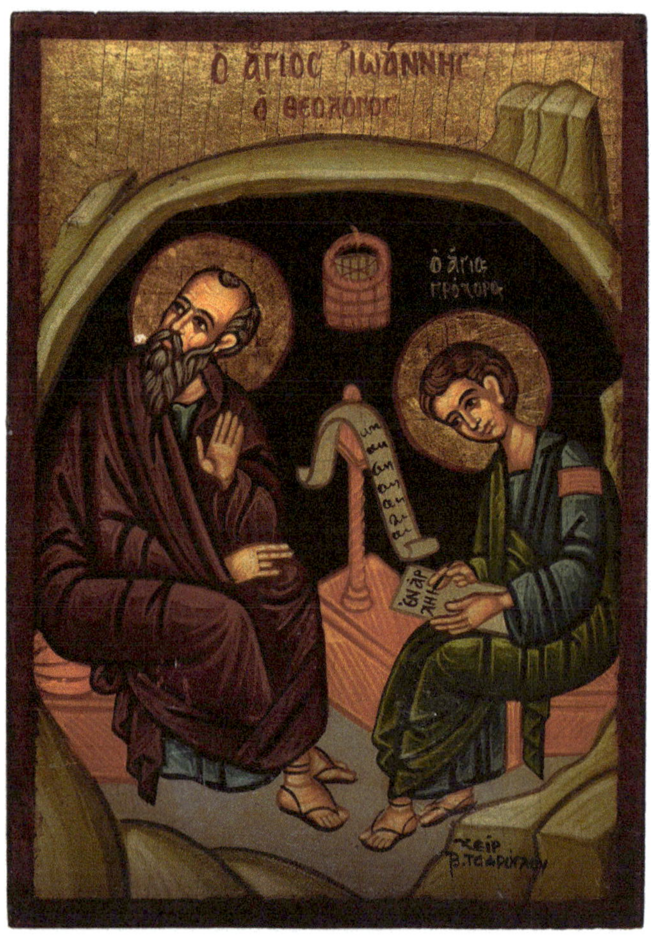

St John and Prochorus

2

Sindology

I have ventured to Patmos and Ithaki, both Greek islands, to complete this book. I came to Patmos to write my previous book, *The Journey*, and to Ithaki to write another book, *Don't Give Up: A Story of Hope in Twelve Golden Rules*. I have returned hopefully to produce for you a coherent treatise which you will enjoy. Patmos is the Isle of St John, the beloved disciple who sat next to Christ at the Last Supper. He was present at the crucifixion, he arrived at the tomb with Peter when resurrection was rumoured, he wrote the book of Revelation and was the only disciple to not be put to death. My journey to Patmos was full of wonderful coincidences that the great Swiss psychologist Carl Gustav Jung would refer to as synchronicity. To get to Patmos from Edinburgh, my starting point, I had to fly to Athens, via London, stay overnight in Athens and then, the following evening, catch the ferry at 7 p.m. to Patmos, arriving at 3.15 a.m. You have to be keen to do this trip!

The last time I was in Athens I visited three churches, all of significance to me and all now sadly closed. This time proved different. I walked down to Plaka, found some great icon shops, one in particular, but I kept my wallet firmly in my pocket. I then, after some directions, found the ancient church of St John the Theologian, and then the Exarchate Church of the Holy Sepulchre of Jerusalem. This is the only other place in the world to have the extremely strange (to a scientist, such as myself, and I think perhaps for non-scientists as well) ceremony of Jerusalem fire. This takes place at Easter, in both Athens and Jerusalem. In Jerusalem, the Patriarch enters Christ's tomb, wearing a white garment with no pockets, and holding two candles. He has no matches, lighters, or any other fire-creating equipment; he is searched to preclude "cheating" and enters the tomb, which is locked behind him. Every year his candles light spontaneously with a light which does not burn. He then emerges and passes the light to the Armenian Patriarch and then the Coptic Patriarch. From there it passes to the people who all have candles, and they pass it from hand to hand. This is not normal light; people pass it over their hair and faces, and nobody has ever been burnt.

After exploring this church, I then visited the main cathedral, something I have always missed, a nineteenth-century structure with a very beautiful interior. I thereafter returned to our hotel and picked up my mother, and off we went to the Museum of Byzantine Art, a great gallery and a wonderful lunch venue. There, to my absolute delight, was an extra exhibition of icons from the Tetryakov Gallery in Moscow, with a couple of Rublevs. More on him later! The Tetryakov Gallery many years ago kindly granted me permission to use one of their pictures for the front cover of my book *Women's Cancers: Pathways to Healing*. What an amazing start to a trip where you intend to write a book on icons!

One of the other stimuli to many of these travels came from a book written by Paul Badde, *The True Icon: From the Shroud of Turin to the Veil of Manoppello*, published originally in German in 2010. This is a spectacular book for those interested in what has been termed "Sindology". It is one of those rare books you pick up by chance in a bookshop that makes you understand things differently. I personally had never given the Turin Shroud a moment's thought until I walked into the cathedral at the Palais de Papes in Avignon about a decade ago, and there in a side chapel was a copy of the Shroud of Turin. I found it profoundly moving and over the next few years I read various books about it. There is no doubting that it is scientifically completely inexplicable; there is a faint image on a very large piece of cloth many metres long. However, when seen in photographic negative, a positive image of a face and body appears.

An explanation for the generation who only know digital cameras: until the 1980s we used to take photos and the image went on to a spool of film in the camera. Once you had taken your thirty-six photos or however big the spool was, you wound the film into the spool, removed it from the camera and took it to the developers. A few days later you collected or were sent your photos. No deleting the not so good ones: you were lumbered with what you had taken, good, bad and indifferent. However, in the back of the folder which contained your photos were the negatives, i.e. the reverse light images, always ghostly and sometimes funny.

The Turin Shroud has been displayed and venerated by the faithful occasionally every century since it was brought to Western Europe after the sack of Constantinople by the Fourth Crusade in 1204. However, it was only in 1898 that the photographic negative image was discovered. The face is contused, the body scourged, the hands and feet show a body crucified, and there is a hole in the side of the thorax. These are, of course, all the injuries associated with the Gospel descriptions of Christ's crucifixion. We know that the Byzantine Emperor Manuel I Comnenus (1148–1180) showed it to a delegation from Hungary in 1150. We also know it was associated with Hagia Sophia in Istanbul (Constantinople).

Another venerated item is known as the Cloth of Edessa, or St Veronica's Cloth, the Veil of Manoppello or the Mandylion. There is much dispute as to whether St Veronica existed. One story tells us that, as Christ carried his cross through Jerusalem, she handed the piece of cloth to Jesus to wipe his face and the miraculous image was imprinted. The other, to my mind, more likely explanation, is that this was another of the burial cloths traditionally used, in this case the face cloth. It is also worth noting that Veronica is an anagram of vera icon (true icon). When one visits Hagia Sophia, there are mosaic images that bear a striking resemblance to the Veil of Manoppello. As soon as you see this image you know it is the forerunner of all the iconographic images, and this is also where the term "not made by human hands" comes from. This cloth has also been subjected to much scientific analysis. As with the Shroud, there is no explanation for it; it is not made from dyes or paints. This is a big area of study by scientists who are referred to as sindologists. It is a difficult area to work in for fear of ridicule by one's fellow scientists and possible hatred from some believers.

The New Testament basis for sindology is from John 20:1–8. There is some discussion among biblical scholars as to who the "other disciple, the one whom Jesus loved" might be, and some say that he is none other than St John himself:

> Early on the first day of the week, while it was still dark, Mary Magdalene came to the tomb and saw that the stone had been

> removed from the tomb. So she ran and went to Simon Peter and the other disciple, the one whom Jesus loved, and said to them, 'They have taken the Lord out of the tomb, and we do not know where they have laid him.' Then Peter and the other disciple set out and went towards the tomb. The two were running together, but the other disciple outran Peter and reached the tomb first. He bent down to look in and saw the linen wrappings lying there, but he did not go in.
>
> Then Simon Peter came, following him, and went into the tomb. He saw the linen wrappings lying there.

This is a powerful reminder that there were perceived to be two ritually unclean but vital cloths known to the inner circle of the early church.

In recent years, there has been considerable debate about the genuineness of the shroud. However, there are also always those who choose to regard it as a sacred object.

We are now going follow the path of the Cloth of Edessa.

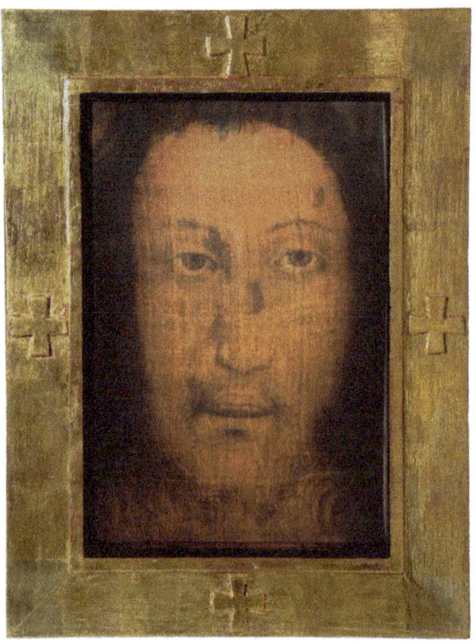

The Cloth of Edessa

3

Constantinople—Istanbul

Deborah and I flew from Terminal 5 Heathrow to Ataturk Airport, Istanbul, arriving mid-afternoon to find it overcast and cold. A taxi quickly whisked us to the Sultan Ahmet area and then, with some difficulty, to our hotel. The Sultan Ahmet area is quite a maze and the Hotel Sultania has no direct road access. The hotel has been designed to make you feel like a Sultan, and in this and many other features it goes a long way towards succeeding. Our room had a somewhat risqué picture covering the bathroom door of a scene from the harem; a scantily clad woman in high heels was being washed by a servant. I commented to the porter, "This is every man's dream!"

We settled into our room and unpacked before we made the short walk up the hill above the hotel to reach Hagia Sophia, the Blue Mosque and the Topkapi Palace. All of these sites were closed, but it was just great to soak up the atmosphere of the area and this amazing city. We visited the odd shop and spent much time in an English-language bookshop with a great selection of books, which were unfortunately very expensive, my favourite being £250—not a runner! The owner had studied architecture in London but was unable to find work back home in Istanbul and had opened his bookshop instead. It was mostly Christian books that were on sale. Bearing in mind his selection of books I was slightly surprised to find that he himself was a Muslim, but this was a city of surprises. He did me the favour of selling me a CD of Sufi chant, which was most interesting, but more on this later.

We returned to our room and, after a swift beer, rested and then, glory be, slept! I had bought two books—*The Bridge: A Journey between Orient and Occident* and *Constantinople*—at Daunt in Marylebone, just the best bookshop for travellers on the planet. The first book I tackled was *The*

Bridge, written by a Dutchman, Geert Mak, and very clever it was, a mix of modern observation interspersed with history, all centred on the Galata bridge which runs from Old Constantinople across the Golden Horn to what was new Constantinople. I had started it on the plane and finished it that evening.

Following the little sleep, we had dinner in the hotel's rooftop restaurant. Meze and kebab, washed down with good local gin, a decent wine and finished off, literally and metaphorically in my case, with a Metaxa brandy. We then repaired to bed for a big sleep.

Breakfast the following morning consisted of fruit, omelette, orange and coffee. Our trip out commenced with a rip-off taxi ride but did allow us the complete circle of old Constantinople, seeing the massive Theodosian walls; they make our castles in the UK look like pimples. The huge fortress covered maybe three or four miles and we passed through the massive walls to the church of St Saviour in Chore. This is now a museum, but there has been a church here for 1,500 years, the current incarnation dating from around AD 1100. What beautiful architecture, with just amazing Byzantine ceilings!

The fall of Constantinople in 1453 was one of those seismic shifts in history which marked the end of an era, in this case the Roman Empire. Constantinople, its capital, had been undergoing a process of contraction over many centuries. There had been an ever-increasing Ottoman incursion into the previous empire. Sultan Mehmet II, then only twenty-one years of age, had built a massive fortress only a few miles from the city. There had been many previous sieges, the Byzantines much helped by the possession of Greek Fire, an incendiary weapon frequently used to set fire to approaching ships. However, in 1453, despite much effort having been made by the Byzantines to garner the support of western Christendom, only the Genoese had come to render assistance. In essence, the defenders were too few and for the Ottoman assailants this was to be their victory. The tale of the Fall has been much written about. Those huge walls repelled the besiegers again and again, but both sides knew the weak spot in the huge fortifications, and that was where it finally gave way, the Emperor Constantine XI Palaeologus and his closest associates all fighting to the death. The Emperor reputedly said, "Is there no Christian to cut off my head?" His own men refused, and he went down by Ottoman swords. History changed that day, the effects of which are still being felt to this time.

I had a plan: this involved walking down the hill to the Golden Horn and finding the Greek Patriarchate. This proved a very bad idea. The area we walked through was very poor and Deborah in her coat of faux black horse fur and my coat designed by Karl Lagerfeld stood out. (I bought the coat in a sale for 75 per cent off. I always call it my Richard Lager-drinker coat; I am partial to the odd beer.) Anyway, we stuck out like sore thumbs on our walk when "heaven" sent a taxi; this was not a regular taxi route, so we were lucky.

We swept by the Greek Patriarchate and Jewish synagogue. I tried to get our grumpy driver to stop but to no avail, and back to Sultan Ahmet we went. I had meant him to stop and wait while we went in, but that wasn't on his agenda. At least he took us the right route, and it was half the price of the outward journey. The best bit was that the driver on the way out had offered to wait for us and no doubt take us back by the previous long route thus tripling the rip-off!

We were deposited near to Hagia Sophia—staggering!

This building started life as the world's greatest cathedral and after the fall of Constantinople it became a mosque. In the twentieth century, it became a museum, which it was at the time we visited. Very controversially it has recently reverted to being a mosque. The whole place takes one's breath away. I am not surprised that when Mehmet II arrived on the day of his conquest to find one of his soldiers digging up the floor, the result was instant death by clubbing or beheading. For this we can give hearty thanks, as here is the original building in all its glory: the sheer size, the 1,500-year, the dome, the demi domes, the mosaics—all take one's breath away. It is worthwhile noting that Mehmet II, when he had built and installed himself in the Topkapi Palace, reckoned that one of his gardeners had stolen a cucumber. No one would admit to the crime, so he had them all (reputedly over twenty of them) disembowelled until he found the culprit! A little extreme to say the least, but I feel very certain there were no more stolen cucumbers.

We emerged into daylight and progressed to the Blue Mosque, which was closed for prayers—wrong timing on our part. So we went to the Hippodrome, an expansive area to the side of the Blue Mosque, where

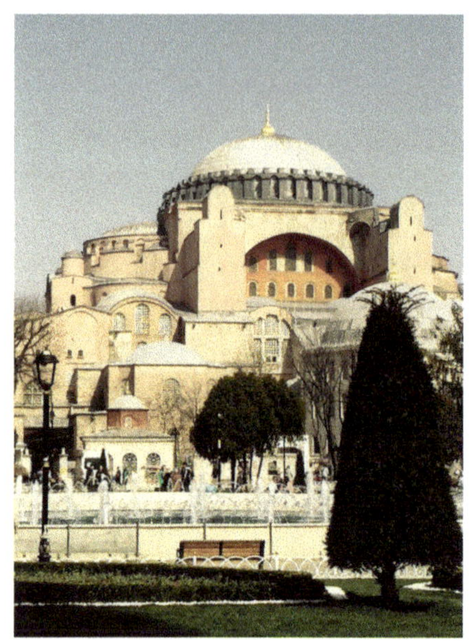

Hagia Sophia

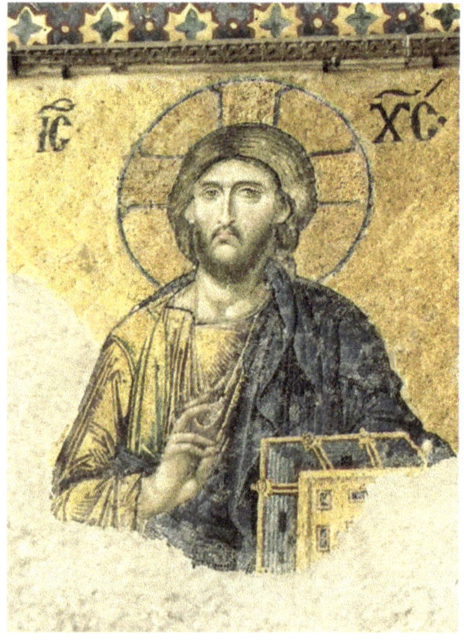

Mosaic of Christ Pantocrator in Hagia Sophia

there are two needles dating back to the time of Constantine and earlier. We then wandered left to a bazaar but retreated back up the hill to find a Turkish Bath. We did, however, become distracted by a new soap shop and another delightful little place called Sufi. In the latter, I bought myself a small cushion. A tasty lunch followed: a little meze, with a good view of the sites and prices high, but that was fair.

Following this we went to the Blue Mosque, shoes off and headgear on for Deborah. This was the first time either of us had been in a mosque. It was very beautiful with wonderful tiling and the biggest expanse of carpet I have ever seen. There was a holiday atmosphere inside with people sitting around on the carpets. We emerged into the daylight, put on our shoes and progressed down the hill. I saw a tray with a painting of Istanbul on it: I was much taken with it, Deborah less so. I came back later, and she was right: it was not hand painted as the price had suggested. In fact, I got something similar at the airport for £12!

We returned to the hotel briefly to drop off our shopping and then we walked down to the Port at the Galata Bridge to join a Bosporus cruise. The walk was chaotic when one approached the port. There were hundreds of people. There were some definite ne'er-do-wells under the bridge, certainly enough to fuel the urban paranoia brought on by Mak's book; the Galata Bridge pickpockets regard themselves as the best on the planet! Crowds of fishermen were there with their rods, just as Mak had described.

Returning to Istanbul: our boat crossed to new Constantinople, also known as Galata, widely regarded as the start of the Orient, then under the bridge and off down the coast. We passed much poverty and squalor, mixed with palaces as big as Versailles, and then we crossed the Bosporus to Asia, where we stopped for two minutes. I was twenty feet away from Asia but not allowed to get off; the seaman did not looking too friendly at my request.

We then returned to the European side and on up the river, under massive suspension bridges and passing the huge fortress built by Mehmet II the year before he conquered the city. The Byzantines could have been in no doubt as to Mehmet's intent, which was to conquer them. Our boat moved back over to the Asian side and then via the Leander lighthouse back to port.

The trip had taken one and a half hours in total, and it had shown us the vastness of the cityscape. On either side of the Bosporus, as we had headed up towards the Black Sea among the poverty of Galata, the houses became bigger and grander, as did the owners' boats. We came back down the Asian side seeing equally grand accommodation. We had a very strong impression that the rich live well away from the centre. I had this confirmed for me recently when the designer Anouska Hempel was reported as kitting out a new palace on the Bosporus at some eye-watering price. One can really understand why the Turks feel in no way second class in comparison to Paris, London, Rome and New York. This is a world city, perhaps the original after Rome.

The walk through the throngs back to the hotel suddenly became much less threatening when my ex-wife donned a headscarf tightly round her head—all hassles disappeared. It was funny because I look Mediterranean and when on my own encountered no trouble at all, whereas with Deborah it became a little wearing. That evening after a rest we returned to the rooftop restaurant for dinner again: gin, wine, Metaxa, accompanying beautiful fried ravioli, prawns and onion mash.

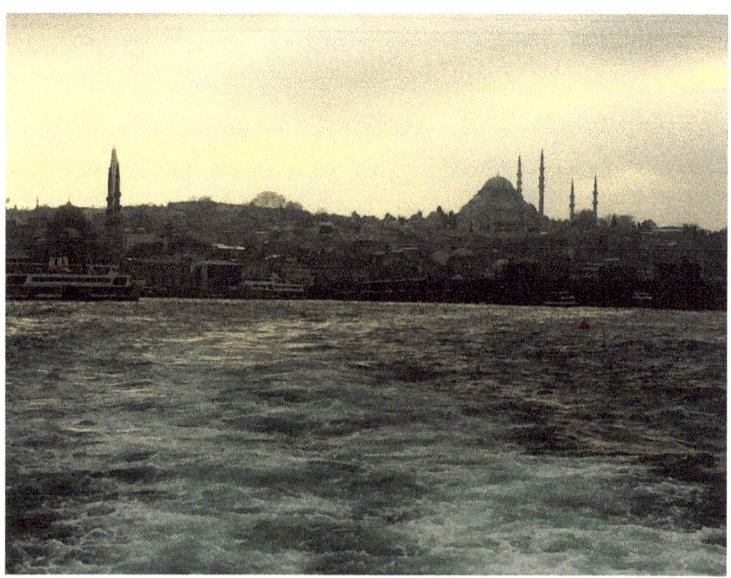

The Bosporus, Istanbul

We retired to bed, and I, with headphones I hasten to add, listened to my Sufi chant CD, which was totally mesmerizing. It was very close to Byzantine chant and even a little similar to Gregorian chant. The Jesus Prayer, the Prayer of the Heart, comes easily with this music; the result was transcendence and off to sleep.

Breakfast the following morning was in the rooftop restaurant. Sultania guests like us mixed with the sister hotel for Turkish guests. Until this point the fact that there were two hotels on the one site had been hidden from us. I speculated whether the hotels were owned and run separately by brothers. They were, but each brother ran both, and also had another hotel.

After breakfast we climbed the hill to the Topkapi Palace: the Sultan's palace. We walked past innumerable Byzantine columns and column heads, some similar in design to the one in our little Greek garden at home. This is the name I gave to our little six by twelve feet footwell in front of the house. It is whitewashed in the Greek style and full of flowers and herbs, thyme, lavender, sage and bay. We also have a copy of the head of a Byzantine column kindly created for me by Alex Milne, a Scottish master stonemason. Alex has a remarkable skill in fashioning stone, and he worked on the restoration of King James VI of Scotland's banqueting chamber at Stirling Castle.

Many years ago, when Deborah and I went through a very sad time, Alex kindly constructed a small monument for us at the south end of the Isle of Bute. It was designed by my old schoolfriend Gordon McEachern and executed by Alex. I can still see Alex running across Garroch Head with a wheelbarrow full of rocks. I little realized just how strong he was until a few years later when I commissioned him to build a replica of the chapel of Agios Andreas, on the island of Ithaki. I sent him the photos, and a few months later he phoned to tell me that the "model" in stone was ready. It was intended for the little Greek garden at the house in Scotland.

On my next trip to Scotland, I passed by his house to collect it. In the garage, he showed me the structure, which is approximately 18" by 12" by 20". It was a perfect replica. Alex then said he would put it in the boot of my car. I watched as he bent down to lift it. Now Alex is small in height, as I am, but sadly for me and happily for him immensely stronger. I watched him slowly carry it to my car with growing alarm. He placed it in the boot, and the whole of the back of the car dropped down, a pretty substantial car at that. I instantly realized that if I braked heavily for any reason the "chapel" would fall straight through the car, and I knew I had no chance of lifting it out of the boot myself. I am a typical surgeon in my middle years, I hope, with a bad back on and off. Anyway, I got down to Bute without incident, and Duncan Whitelaw, a local farmer and a man of great strength, kindly helped me, by lifting it and placing it on the front patio, and there it remains! A better resting place anyway than that which had been planned. This manoeuvre planted a little piece of Greece in the west of Scotland.

Ithaki, in western Greece, is another remarkable island of transcendent beauty. The wonderful C. P. Cavafy poem sums it up in far better words than I can ever manage. I first visited the island over twenty years ago and have been lucky enough to have been many times, it never loses its appeal:

> As you set out for Ithaka
> hope your road is a long one,
> full of adventure, full of discovery.
> Laistrygonians, Cyclops,
> angry Poseidon—don't be afraid of them:
> you'll never find things like that on your way
> as long as you keep your thoughts raised high,
> as long as a rare excitement
> stirs your spirit and your body.
> Laistrygonians, Cyclops,
> wild Poseidon—you won't encounter them
> unless you bring them along inside your soul,
> unless your soul sets them up in front of you.
> Hope your road is a long one.
> May there be many summer mornings when,
> with what pleasure, what joy,
> you enter harbors you're seeing for the first time;
> may you stop at Phoenician trading stations
> to buy fine things,
> mother of pearl and coral, amber and ebony,

sensual perfume of every kind—
as many sensual perfumes as you can;
and may you visit many Egyptian cities
to learn and go on learning from their scholars.
Keep Ithaka always in your mind.
Arriving there is what you're destined for.
But don't hurry the journey at all.
Better if it lasts for years,
so you're old by the time you reach the island,
wealthy with all you've gained on the way,
not expecting Ithaka to make you rich.
Ithaka gave you the marvelous journey.
Without her you wouldn't have set out.
She has nothing left to give you now.
And if you find her poor, Ithaka won't have fooled you.
Wise as you will have become, so full of experience,
you'll have understood by then what these Ithakas mean.*

This road led to a series of tiers with gardens. It was quite stunning and presumably built atop the old Byzantine emperor's palace. The Veil of Manoppello certainly spent many centuries in the now long-destroyed Imperial Palace Chapel of the Byzantine emperors. It was described as such in the year 1157 by the Danish Abbot Nicholas Bergthorson during the reign of Manuel I Komnenos. During the Crusader sack of the city in 1204, just under fifty years later, the Crusaders knew the religious artefacts of the greatest value to remove! They failed to steal the Crown of Thorns, but more on this later.

The kitchens contained a huge wealth of treasures, presents from European monarchs, although none from the stingy Brits; they were

---

* C. P. Cavafy, "The City" from *C.P. Cavafy: Collected Poems*. Translated by Edmund Keeley and Philip Sherrard. Translation Copyright © 1975, 1992 by Edmund Keeley and Philip Sherrard. Reproduced with permission of Princeton University Press. There is a lovely recording of this on YouTube by the late Sir Sean Connery and Vangelis, which is well worth a listen: <https://www.youtube.com/watch?v=i8is5ZE4_CUM>, accessed 2 December 2021.

mostly French, Polish, German and Russian. The entrance reception had large couches similar to those I had seen in Qatar. The next part of the palace contained innumerable artefacts including many receptacles containing the Prophet's beard, the sword of King David, the cooking pot of Abraham and the Rod of Moses.

From there we went on to the Hall of the Ambassadors, and then to the Harem. Deborah described this as the fanciest prison she had seen, but it was still a prison. At its height, there were a few wives and a thousand concubines, guarded by a large cohort of eunuchs: again, it was quite extraordinarily luxurious with views across the city, the Golden Horn and the Bosporus.

We left the palace, and Deborah headed for the finest Turkish baths in town, next to Hagia Sophia. I went back to the hotel, completed our packing and checked us out. The bags went into storage, and I headed back up the hill and visited the Cistern, a huge underground colonnaded area approximately 200 metres by 50. Most of the columns were plain, but there are two carved Medusa columns and one carved with tears being shed down it. Remarkably, this was all hidden for a thousand years; it was then discovered that householders in the area had holes in their floors from which they could draw fresh water and even occasionally fish. The sixth-century emperor Justinian had built the cisterns, which were supplied via aqueducts from lakes twenty miles away. The cisterns were opened up and the water used, and in 1985 they were restored to their present-day appearance.

From there, I went back through the Hippodrome, returned to the Sufi shop and bought Deborah and Catrina presents of Kilim cushions, very attractive to my mind and happily, as it transpired later, to theirs. I then found my daughters Madeleine and Lara a little elephant and whirling dervish. Just around the corner I sat down to a meze in the restaurant opposite our hotel. Deborah joined me for a light lunch, and then we headed to the airport.

We had an uneventful flight home, if somewhat delayed, which became more interesting when we arrived at Heathrow. A fellow in a red cap from British Border Control was waiting at the door and told the stewards there would be a passport check at the top of the steps. As I got there, I was greeted by two suited men, who looked like plain clothes police. One looked at my passport and said, "Welcome home, sir," not the language of Border Control at all. It then became clear that the whole place was staked out with eleven policemen, waiting no doubt for a potential terrorist in our midst.

Reflection

Istanbul is quite a place. The original world city was very much more impressive than I had ever imagined. This is a city of high rank: nowadays London, Paris and New York I think would be regarded as the top three, with Rome and Istanbul in the next tier, the cities of the first millennium. I found myself dreaming of the place for the first two nights after we came home, a sure sign that it had made a deep impression on me.

I have been reading *Constantinople* by Edmondo De Amicis and do wonder if C. S. Lewis read this book; I'm sure both he and J. R. R. Tolkien did. The Gondor of Middle Earth bears some comparisons to the Constantinople of yesteryear, and Tashbaan in the Narnia books is a clear description of Istanbul after the fall of Constantinople. This includes the description of the Galata Bridge and the world crossing it, the tiered structure of the city, as well as its political organization. I can only speculate that this was much discussed by the authors, perhaps over a pint in the Eagle and Child, their Oxford boozer and favoured watering hole of the Inklings, a group of like-minded people the most famous of whom were J. R. R. Tolkien, C. S. Lewis and Charles Williams. I cannot help but wonder if they ever visited Istanbul. I always speculated when walking with Andrew on Mount Athos whether the duo had visited there or read about it. However, I have no doubt they were much influenced by it.

Regarding icons, the Cloth of Edessa, the Turin Shroud and many relics, including the Crown of Thorns, were kept before increasing financial problems prompted various emperors to sell relics at a high cost to Western Europe, after which the Fourth Crusade (1202–4) plundered the city. The Crown of Thorns was saved from the Crusaders but later sold for a king's ransom by the Byzantine emperor to the French King Louis IX, who built Sainte-Chapelle as its reliquary chapel in 1248. This relic is today the property of Notre Dame Cathedral; mercifully it was saved from the terrible fire of 2019, and since then it has been housed in the Louvre.

I was once at a conference in Paris, and in the break in the afternoon, decided to go to Sainte-Chapelle, probably the finest reliquary chapel ever built. When you enter the chapel, it appears to be floating on air. It is in the Gothic style, but its supporting pillars are much more finely constructed than in previous church buildings. Between the pillars lies the most exquisite stained glass; the effect is awesome.

That day, as I approached, the question in my mind was where is the Crown of Thorns now? In fact, when I got to the entrance to the chapel there was a massive queue, and I knew I did not have enough time to wait. I decided to walk around the corner to Notre Dame Cathedral where to my enormous surprise there was a poster advertising "The Veneration of the Crown of Thorns" at 3 p.m. every first Friday of the month, i.e. the following day. It transpires that during the French revolution the chapel handed the Crown to the Knights of Jerusalem for safekeeping. They were based 400 yards away at Notre Dame. A very moving ceremony followed the next day and I, for one, kissed the glass cylindrical tube containing the Crown. I have to confess to taking a quick peek at the thorns, which are truly fearsome. These are no brier or rose thorns as I had always imagined; they are 4-cm-plus spikes!

To return to Constantinople: the French, English, Scottish and German knights must have been in total disbelief when they saw the wealth and grandeur of the city. It is estimated that it housed 500,000 people in the Middle Ages, compared to 45,000 in London, less than 100,000 in Paris and maybe 15,000 in Edinburgh. I returned staggered by the place, coming from modern London and knowing New York well.

The greatness that was once Constantinople can still be experienced today, to a degree, not only in the city itself but also in Mystras in the Peloponnese Region of mainland Greece. This was where the Byzantine court, or what was left of it, fled after the fall of the city.

The late Maria Andipa, icon expert and owner of the Andipa Gallery in Chelsea, London, supporter of the Friends of Mount Athos and past president of the London Hellenic Society, had told me about it a few years ago, having just visited herself. I was fortunate to have a medical colleague and friend, Dr Angeliki Rouvali, who moved back to Greece after undertaking medical training at Imperial College. She kindly facilitated a splendid trip to this site near Sparta, which is an amazing concentration of churches, palaces and monasteries. It is no coincidence that, of all the beautiful sites of Greece, this is often used for the front covers of guidebooks. I cannot help but take you a little further into this amazing place.

The opportunity came to visit when I was in Ithaki on summer holiday. The ferry journey took two and a half hours, Ithaki just visible in the haze in the distance as we came into Astakos' waters. There was a smooth transfer into my Nissan Micra hire car. I had a light breakfast before I left and then drove off down to Mesolongi and the lagoons there. This is the place where Byron died, possibly of malaria, unsurprisingly in such a low-lying area, although it is quite pretty in some respects these days. I suspect it was not pretty when Byron was there. He is still a national hero in Greece, but I failed to find the Byron Museum and kept going on to the motorway down over the Patras Bridge, a truly splendid piece of engineering that crosses the mouth of the Gulf of Corinth. It is a long drop down from the bridge, and there are still plenty of people taking the ferries that run across to save the bridge toll, which is €13.50; to put it in perspective, that is equal to all the motorway tolls the whole way from Missolongi to Athens. As you leave the bridge, you turn left and go along the north side of the Peloponnese, on the south side of the Gulf of Corinth.

I drove to Athens, making a good pace up the motorway. I passed one car in disbelief: the driver was lying back in his seat with his foot out of the window, clearly texting and not even looking at the road, doing probably 75 mph in the middle lane.

I arrived in central Athens smoothly and went directly to the hotel, without becoming lost. The only place I went wrong was a favourite trick of mine, taking the wrong turn at the point where the hotel was visible.

I went to the Hilton and had a sleep before meeting Angeliki for drinks and dinner. We had drinks in the Galaxy Bar, and as hoped for, we watched the sun go down to the right of the Acropolis. We had meant to walk down to Plaka, but as it was getting a bit late a taxi seemed preferable, which dropped us in Syntagma Square, and from there we wandered down to a truly delightful restaurant. I was being very spoilt; the food was astoundingly good. We sat in a small courtyard, and church bells rang throughout dinner—I had arrived on the Feast of the Virgin Mary, which is Greece's biggest public holiday. I must admit I rather like the sound of bells myself. It was a tapas-style meal with much interesting conversation. I certainly felt very fortunate to be Angeliki's guest.

The following morning after breakfast I got into my car, set the satnav for Angeliki's address and duly drove up the hill above the hotel. This proved hard work: I had a little cramp in my left foot from too much clutch work. There are very steep hills in Athens, and I wasn't wearing boots but flip-flops; in addition, I hadn't adjusted the seat properly. Anyway, Angeliki was waiting. She had brought a picnic, and we bowled off through Athens. She pointed out where her mother had originally come from and had been brought up; at both places there had been fields and farm animals. It is now all heavily built up and near the new Olympic Stadium. We then went down on to the motorway which runs around the north of Athens. Athens has a similar motorway system to Glasgow, effectively one motorway running round the north and one round the south. From there, we bowled along with the Saronic Gulf on the left. Arriving in Corinth we crossed the Corinthian canal: new Corinth lies over to the right; old Corinth lies further up the hill. On this occasion, for the first time ever for me, we turned left to go down into the Peloponnese. It is a fascinating area: rough country, very like Scotland with high mountains, and the valleys are filled with vineyards, fields filled with golden crops and much industrious agriculture. As we were bowling along, I looked down to check that I had plenty of fuel and was reassured to see I had three bars left on the meter, but as we went up a hill, I suddenly felt the car miss a beat and looked again. The car was registering no fuel and the warning light was on, filling me with anxiety. I didn't confess to Angeliki that I had felt the car judder; she was very reassuring that there was a filling station probably within five miles, and thankfully she was right. She knows the area very well because, as part of her medical training, she had been sent to this remote area to practise as a GP. She was sent to Monemvasia, a Byzantine village down on the coast in the Southern Peloponnese, but she covered a big area, regularly being called to fatal road traffic accidents. This didn't surprise me particularly, having seen similar accidents in rural Scotland and also observing a lot of driving! We dropped down through the Peloponnese with its soaring high mountains, birds of prey wheeling amid rocky outcrops high above, which reminded me of Glen Coe in Scotland. We came off the motorway heading for Sparta, which is now the modern city below Mystras. I had looked in the guidebook, and there are some fairly poor ancient remains at Sparta, but this was not the purpose of this day's visit. Mystras was our goal.

Mystras is regarded as the most authentic Byzantine site in Greece. This was a city built around 1100 when the Byzantine Empire was undoubtedly in some degree of decline, but it was still about 300 years before the fall of Constantinople. This of course occurred after the long-term retraction of Byzantine power and lands which were reduced to little more than the city of Constantinople. Before Constantinople fell, the Emperor, Constantine XI, managed to get many of his family, and the royal court, out of the city by boat. They travelled to Mystras, which was where the court resided for I think the next fifty years before the Ottomans caught up with them in about 1500. The Byzantine Court came to an end, but its presence can still be felt there, even today.

Mystras itself is rather like the holy area in Lebanon, with multiple churches and monasteries dotting the hillside, here all dating from 1150–1200, a truly memorable sight. It took us two and a half hours to get there, and we parked and looked up the hill. There was a huge castle on the top of the hill, and I commented, "I don't fancy climbing up there!" There was another castle about halfway up the hill. Little did I realize we would actually be climbing all the way to that level. It was not that far but it was a very hot day. It is an interesting site and, in some respects, similar in layout to Delphi in that you slowly but surely wander uphill, taking in more and more sights as you go. It starts with the cathedral; there is a square in its floor showing a Byzantine double-headed eagle. It is believed the last emperor was crowned on that spot. There are also icons showing the last emperor meeting his death outside the walls of Constantinople. There was a small museum which had some quite interesting stonework and also fragments of clothing and a shoe from the Byzantine Court. It looked pretty much like a shoe that would dress an elegant lady today, although apparently their shoes had neither right nor left—ambidextrous shoes!

From there we wandered up, exploring some small chapels in which many of the frescos had sadly faded. Further up the hill we came to the only currently active monastery. I had texted Angeliki to see whether this was a long-trouser or short-trouser site, but in fact I had packed both, and when we arrived at the site it was clear everybody was in shorts. We decided that if they wanted us to cover up, they would undoubtedly supply material to allow us to do that. Funnily enough, there was a sign saying material would be supplied, but in fact it was not. The church interior itself was beautiful and certainly brought back to me the monastery of St John the Divine in Patmos and my previous Athonite experiences.

From there we climbed up the hill to the Royal Palace, but this area was closed for refurbishment.

We then came down the hill, and by this time it was 4.30. We had a table booked at the Athens Hilton for dinner at nine and decided that we would eat our picnic in the car. We decided against driving to the castle at the very top but instead to head for Athens. With the big public holiday, we had hit some traffic jams leaving Athens, but we encountered none of those on the way back, and we were in Athens just after 7.

I dropped Angeliki at her house, so she could have a shower and change, and I went back to the Hilton, had a much-needed shower and changed for dinner. I had been dreaming of cold beer during the long walk and duly ordered this to the room, drinking it with great relish. Angeliki arrived in the foyer at 8.30. It is worthwhile saying the Hilton had only been reopened for a week or two and normally was bustling and busy, but in fact on this stay it was mostly empty. I do not think they had more than 100 guests in the entire hotel. I think they have twelve floors with 100 rooms a floor possibly, so it was very quiet. The main restaurant was shut, but we managed a splendid repast of sushi washed down with the wonderful Santorinian wine Assyrtiko. This restaurant, I may say, converted me to the joys of sushi a few years ago.

I had managed to square up my chasing of Byzantium to an even better degree now, satisfying my desire to trace the Byzantine Court back to Mystras.

Many of you may will have read Patrick Leigh Fermor's books describing his walk from London to Constantinople in the 1930s. This is travelogue at its best, but he never quite gets to Constantinople. His story is similar to *The Way of a Pilgrim*, in which the pilgrim never quite reaches Jerusalem. Leigh Fermor (known to his friends as Paddy) was involved in the SOE-organized capture of General Heinrich Kreipe, the German Commander of Crete in the Second World War. Leigh Fermor, William Moss and Cretan partisans, dressed in German uniform, captured Kreipe and with Major Ciclitera and much help from local partisans spirited him across Crete and away to Alexandria, at great risk to themselves. My friend and colleague, Rick Keays, an anaesthetist, used to visit Kardomyli regularly, where Leigh Fermor lived until he died at the age of ninety-six. Rick was in a restaurant when an elderly lady collapsed, and he helped to resuscitate her. It transpired that she was an ex-girlfriend of the redoubtable Paddy. This I suspect did not make her unique. I have felt a great debt to Leigh Fermor: he is one of those authors who, once you read one of his books, you have to read them all and you are always sorry to finish them. In a further coincidence, Major Ciclitera's son is a physician and used to practise from the room opposite to mine at the Lister Hospital in West London.

Returning to my thoughts after the trip to Istanbul, Sufi chant has proved a revelation, although not a surprising one. Repetitive prayer crosses the religious divide from Orthodox Christians to Sufi Muslims, Jewish sects, Hindus and Buddhists, and so there was no surprise that the Prayer came to me readily when listening to the CD of chant. (When I say readily, I mean within seconds, not the usual few minutes warm-up normally required.)

Continuing the theme of God and music, I am a huge fan of J. S. Bach and his Baroque contemporaries. They sought God through their music. They referred to the music of the spheres, and their music is highly mathematical. I find it very soothing when it is played in the operating theatre and have been lucky to work with anaesthetist colleagues, particularly Dr Geoff Lockwood, who felt the same way. I was very lucky in 2002 when I moved to the Hammersmith hospital. At the time, I was about halfway through my consultant career and had changed hospitals from the beautiful Chelsea and Westminster to the newly formed West

London Gynaecological Cancer Centre. I didn't wholly want to move, leaving behind many good friends at the old hospital, but I was a victim of the Calman Hine report, which rationalized cancer services in the UK. In West London, there were four cancer centres, and they had to become two! This was bound to cause much pain for those involved and it did. However, some of my pain was relieved by walking into theatre in my new hospital to find a familiar face at the top of the table, namely Geoff. We had been senior registrars together in Watford in the early 1990s. We had always got on well, Geoff practising wonderfully gentle and effective anaesthesia always accompanied by Baroque music. He has over the years much expanded my collection of CDs by his example. He and I share a belief that anything after 1800 is usually a bit too modern, though there are exceptions! It certainly works in the operating theatre to maintain calm.

(For the record, I do wholly recognize that the Calman Hine report did get it right. The newly formed, much bigger centres have allowed for much more rapid advances in overall cancer care, perhaps the only loss being slightly more fragmented care.)

My children are driven a bit potty by this baroque music, because if I have had a stressful day at work, J. S. Bach is always first choice in the evening for relaxing music at dinner. Now you do feel sorry for them!

I love the story of a person who asked J. S. Bach: "Papa Bach, how do you manage to compose so much music?" He replied that his music was like a spring of water, it just flowed out of him in an unstoppable fashion. He wrote his wonderful cantatas on a weekly basis once he knew how big his choir was going to be the following week.

It is a funny coincidence, but the day of our return was the first time I experienced the Vicar of Little Venice, Father Gary's, new liturgy, a cunning mix of Brother Roger of Taizé and Le Bec-Hellouin, the Roman Catholic monastery in Normandy visited by many high Anglicans. Much of the service is now sung, which cleverly crosses the multinational nature of our church, which is British, Greek, Italian, American and other nationalities in equal measure. Fr Gary's experiment is bold, and I think will prove successful. Prayerfulness is all!

In my past travels to Mount Athos, the Holy Mountain in Greece, I had stayed in Byzantine monasteries which have been unchanged for centuries, but by travelling to Istanbul I really felt that I had got under the skin of the centre of Byzantium. I could see how all the valuable relics of Christendom would have been here and the enormous jealousy this and the huge wealth of the city would have engendered. There is no excuse for what the Western Latin Crusaders did! Instead of their stated intent of freeing the Holy Land from Muslim domination they sacked the centre of Christendom instead, hence Pope John Paul II's 2004 apology to Orthodox Christians: "In particular, we cannot forget what happened in the month of April 1204. How can we not share, at a distance of eight centuries, the pain and disgust?" In the process they brought much wealth back to Western Europe, particularly to Venice and Rome. This included knives and forks for eating (originally described by the Crusaders as effeminate), good food and of course the Veil of Manoppello and the Shroud of Turin.

Perhaps the greatest injustice was, and continues to be, although to a lesser extent, the airbrushing of the Byzantine historical legacy. So much was written on what happened to the glories of ancient Greece and the suggestion was that ancient Greece just disappeared politically into nothingness. Of course, the truth is that those ideas and culture melded into the Roman Empire. However, while this failed in the West centred upon Rome, it re-arose in the East centred upon Constantinople from the fourth century on. In the early seventh century, the official language changed from Latin to Greek. In this great city was a civilization far beyond what the West had achieved. So why the airbrush? My own belief is that the combination of the Crusader sack of Constantinople, coupled with the West's pathetic effort to come to their Greek Byzantine counterparts' assistance in their hour of need, namely the final siege, left a great feeling of guilt. Western Europe was greatly endangered after the Fall of Constantinople, and many of the ensuing wars might have been avoided if timely assistance had been rendered in 1453 and the preceding years. This is not to denigrate the later Venetian contribution, but rather to place responsibility further west. Of course, it was those further west who came to write the history.

4

Rome and Manoppello

My friend Andrew Wakeham-Dawson and I set off for Rome and began our trip by me making the extremely naïve, in fact stupid, decision to take our hire car into the centre of Rome. Notwithstanding this, we were doing extremely well until we arrived on a major street which we thought led from our motorway into town. However, half an hour later, instead of being in the centre of town we were in fact right outside Rome all over again. We appeared to have gone, if you imagine a clock, to 3 o'clock, and then back out at 1 o'clock, so we had done a big curve through the northern part of the city; there was no satnavs for us.

It was time to regroup and reread the map, and this time around we found the right street and successfully followed it all the way to within about a mile of our hotel. There, unfortunately, was a mass student demonstration taking place which seriously delayed us. We finally got to our hotel to discover that parking was difficult to find and the street had been dug up; it took us another hour to park the car. We then discovered that we were almost certainly going to receive some sort of ticket for driving within Rome without the appropriate permit. Having parked up and settled into our respective rooms, we got our boots on and went on a brilliant walking tour through Rome from our hotel at the Piazza del Popolo. We saw the Spanish Steps, we visited innumerable churches, we saw the Pantheon, and the Pizza Navona, and then we crossed the Tiber to the castle of St Angelo.

We gained admittance to the Vatican, by no means a certainty on my part since there are signs precluding you from carrying a penknife. I had a penknife in my pocket which I have always have had, but occasionally these days it proves troublesome. I switched it to my money belt with my pen, which allowed me to get into the Vatican without losing yet another knife. My breach of the legal requirements was stimulated by our having queued for twenty minutes before we found any sign that said you could not have a penknife. Once into St Peter's vast basilica, I realized that I had forgotten how big a church it actually is. Much of the time these days it feels more like a museum, but this is a difficult tightrope walk for all the world's great cathedrals, balancing revenue-producing tourism with worship. The main altar was roped off and there were thousands of people milling around. I unfortunately had the stark choice between partaking in a Mass or going to see the Tomb of St Peter. It had been on my agenda to see the Tomb of St Peter for some time, so I decanted downstairs. It is remarkable how often there are announcements for people to remain silent when the tour guides are telling people in all the languages of the world about what they can see; there is a certain loss of spirituality about the whole experience. St Peter's tomb was very impressive but not nearly as moving as St Francis' tomb in Assisi. St Peter's was set back by perhaps twenty to thirty feet, visible through glass doors and surrounded by many other popes buried within this crypt of the cathedral. In contrast, at St Francis' tomb, pilgrims were lying and kneeling to touch the tomb. I emerged from the crypt to the souvenir area where even an ardent souvenir buyer like I am could not find anything I wanted to buy.

I went back into the basilica where the Mass had now ended. I asked if I could go in to light a candle, and the official looked at me rather strangely and said, "You are only allowed to go in if you wanted to pray." I said that was the purpose of my request and he let me go through! It was interesting that there was no capacity within this centre of Roman Catholicism to light a candle at all. Teo Goroszeniuk, good friend and consultant, had asked me if I would light a candle for him and his family if I visited Monte Cassino, which I may do but may not! So I thought to cover all options and to do the same in St Peter's, but this proved to be an impossible task. I did, however, have a few minutes of contemplation before meeting Andrew at the main door at 6 p.m., as we planned. We then went to the Vatican post office where he wrote a card to each of his two sons and posted them off. We then jumped in a taxi back to the hotel.

We did have one further interlude earlier that afternoon where we walked into a church, were shown down to the basement and, having paid two euros for the privilege, were shown what was meant to be the room in which St Paul had lodged for the two years when he was "imprisoned" in Rome, under guard. All the murals from the church have been taken away to a museum, but we certainly got some of the atmosphere that you might expect from such a place. In a similar vein, within the bowels of St Peter's, you can see the original columns of the church that were there around AD 500. There are two columns remaining and some layers of stonework which date from Emperor Constantine of Constantinople's time. I do believe that Constantine, St Peter and St Paul, for that matter, would be pretty amazed by the structure that is now sitting on this site but perhaps also slightly saddened by the lack of spirituality that is in evidence today. (That is not meant to sound holier than thou!)

On return to our hotel, which was an old nunnery now turned into a very splendid establishment, we had a beer in the courtyard and then repaired to our rooms where I made some phone calls, texted various people and then we met for a splendid meal.

What a day! We had certainly been to the site where the Veil had been for many hundreds of years. The Veil was one of the Vatican's great treasures which was described on many occasions until it disappeared from view in 1527. This was the year that Rome was sacked by German Protestant soldiers.

The Route to Manoppello

We had a fascinating day. We had arrived late the previous night in the Abruzzo region and checked into our agro-tourism farmhouse. We got there just in time for dinner having had difficulty following the directions to find the place. We received a very warm welcome and were then served with a large salad washed down with red wine and a lasagne to follow. I thought that our meal was over, but then there were lamb chops and pork sausages, followed by grappa to help the digestion.

I slept well, and after a good breakfast we left the car at the farmhouse and took ourselves up and across the hills for what proved to be a massively over-ambitious walk. We walked uphill for about a thousand feet and over maybe six miles. A small Jack Russell terrier tagged along with us all the way to a hermitage. The poor wee fellow was almost run over by a lunatic Italian driver at one point, who didn't seem particularly bothered. The Hermitage of St Bartholomew, which we think St Benedict used, is certainly situated in an area of very interesting topography, with a ravine and caves alongside it. Our companion the dog disappeared at this juncture, which was a shame; I do love walking with dogs, but no doubt he needed to return home.

The Hermitage of St Bartholomew was very reminiscent of St Francis' *refugio* above Assisi. There was a pool of water in the chapel with a spoon beside it. I picked up some water to cross myself with, and then an entire Italian family, including two young children, came over and did the same. It was clear that everyone knew what to do!

Quite a lot of tourists who were visiting the hermitage had driven to it; we crossed to the other side of the ravine and into some very remote countryside. We walked uphill for a further 2,500 feet to arrive close to Santo Spirito, but we did not reach it. We had jumped across a fast-moving stream, having thrown our rucksacks across to each other. We were about ten minutes away from Santo Spirito but decided that our masterplan of crossing the park was way over-ambitious. It was 3 o'clock in the afternoon, and we had been walking for five hours and were not even halfway to the perceived destination, where a sign made it clear that there was a further 5,000 feet of climbing, much of it above the snow line. Andrew pointed out that he was glad I was able to cope with plans changing according to circumstances. I said that many a military commander had failed because of an inability to change the plan!

We therefore decided to head for Carmanico Terme. We were, however, worried that after a good eight hours of walking we were struggling to reach our new destination. That's the thing about Andrew's and my plans—they are very optimistic! There was a small village about an hour's walk from Carmanico Terme by the name of Decontra, and we arrived there not daring to think there might be a bar or hotel, but in fact there was another agro-tourism farmhouse. A couple who had just come down the mountain, following what looked like a long walk, showed us to where a very charming proprietrix gave both of us cold beer, and tea and cake for Andrew. She told us she only had one room left and that it had a double bed. I said to her that under no circumstances would I share

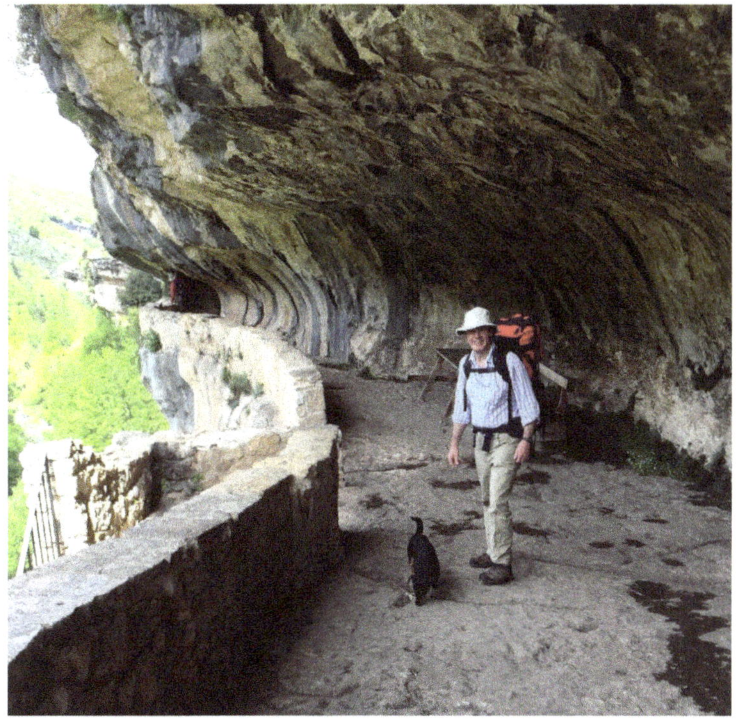

The Hermitage of St Bartholomew and our canine friend

a bed with Andrew and that one of us would sleep on the floor. She then said she would make the couch downstairs up as a bed.

Back in Decontra we sat and had a lovely hour in the sun looking up at the view. In the evening back at the farmhouse, we were told, as approximately twenty of us sat for dinner, that the last people to arrive had to sing a song from their country; unfortunately this looked like the two of us. This was not good as neither of us can sing. However, luck was on our side when two young Italian women from Rome appeared. They were the last and were encouraged to sing, which let us off the hook. There was some fairly heady rough red wine served up in great quantity followed by a huge selection of spirits local to the area. The meal was an enormous affair, starting with pasta with hot chillies, moving on to chicken fried somewhat in the fashion of a veal Milanese with potatoes, chillies and onion, and a vegetable salad with large beans which are a Roman delicacy eaten with pecorino cheese. You had to take two layers of shell from the beans to get to the juicy middle. The proprietrix encouraged singing and there was great merriment around the table. The Italians are a happy people; I think they must have thought it awful when they were posted to Hadrian's Wall or even worse the Antonine Wall. Andrew told me a historical fact I didn't know (not an infrequent event), which was that the Ninth Legion crossed Hadrian's Wall and none ever reappeared, all killed by the Picts. Much closer to our own time, Italian prisoners in the Second World War were sent to Orkney to build the Churchill barricades as part of the defence of the Royal Navy mooring at Scapa Flow. They arrived in that very beautiful, but almost treeless, cold, exposed and windy environment and were not happy. (Not so long ago the roof blew off the hospital from natural causes, not a bomb.) The Italians claimed this was the British equivalent of the Russians sending people into slave labour in Siberia. In fact, though, many of the Italians grew to like it; they built the beautiful Italian chapel from Nissen huts, and there are still visits to this day of Italian families returning to Orkney annually.

All a far cry from where we sat, where I think things have not changed for a very long time. At the end of the long table of people was Grandpa Paul; his grandson, ten-year-old Paul, was serving at table, and at the far end of the table there was a baby. Grandpa Paul was a farmer who at eighty-nine was the same age as my own father, and he took part in the singing. He had worked in Kent planting apples fifty years ago but struggled with Andrew's and my accents. Easy to explain with mine but harder with Andrew's definite Queen's English. On my left was a fellow whose wife was a doctor in Rome. They were both from Rome, and he spoke English, so there was some conversation there.

We now fast forward to the following evening, and we are in Carminico Terme, having made it this time. It is a thermal spa resort high in the Abruzzo mountains. There are many hotels here, but unfortunately virtually all of them were closed.

An amusing point of the day was when the Reverend Doctor (Andrew) put his hand on one of the signs high in the National Park, at which point the entire sign fell to pieces. I was able to accuse the Reverend Doctor of gross vandalism. Having said this, he did manage to put the sign back together.

We got up that morning in our agro-tourism farmhouse and had our breakfast at 8 o'clock. We were gone by just after 9 and walked from Decontra down to Carminico Terme, which took us about an hour. The town is a thermal spa resort high in the Abruzzo mountains. We then tried to find a hotel which was open; there were many but all the ones in the guidebook that we found were in fact closed. The winter season here had ended, but the summer season was due to begin at the end of May. We eventually found a hotel, and I ended up in a little single-bedded room which was perfectly comfortable with a view of the fire escape, always reassuring if one wants to get out in a hurry! Andrew dumped his rucksack completely. I emptied my rucksack of much of the stuff that was in it and turned it into a daysack. The sun was shining so there was certainly no need for the all-weather gear that both of us were carrying, and we took off up a gorge, which proved to be a monster eighteen-mile walk. There was a sign saying you should inform the police if you were entering the park, but the police station was closed. The area is interesting: very remote, with the only wild bears left in Western Europe and also, reputedly, wolves. We happily encountered neither of these mammals. I am sure the other reason for registering your presence is that if you had an accident, it would be very difficult to get you out. Amusingly Andrew now had only his binoculars and insect-catching gear. He also looks very English, whereas in every Mediterranean country I am mistaken for a local. So this particular morning Andrew looked like a wealthy English eccentric who had hired a local porter to carry his gear for the day, a very British approach. Suffice to say that as we walked through the town, we got some funny looks!

Andrew's insect-catching equipment has certainly produced some amusement in the past. (Andrew is currently the editor of a journal called *The Entomologist*. This scientific periodical started life in 1864 and has had a number of clergy editors over the years. Andrew was also past Executive Secretary for the International Commission for Zoological Nomenclature at the Natural History Museum.) A few years ago, we were on our way to Mount Athos in northern Greece, when we stopped at a deserted taverna. Only the owner, his wife and a friend were lunching. As Andrew and I enjoyed a soft drink, he pointed out a fly to me. I should say there were many flies around our table. I commented on this, but he

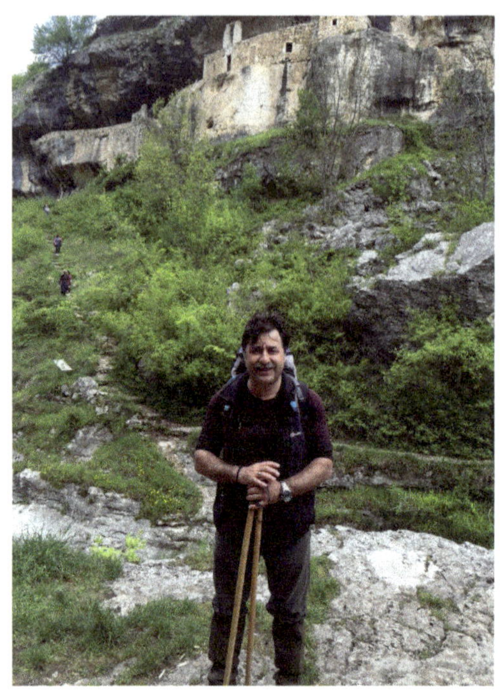

The author

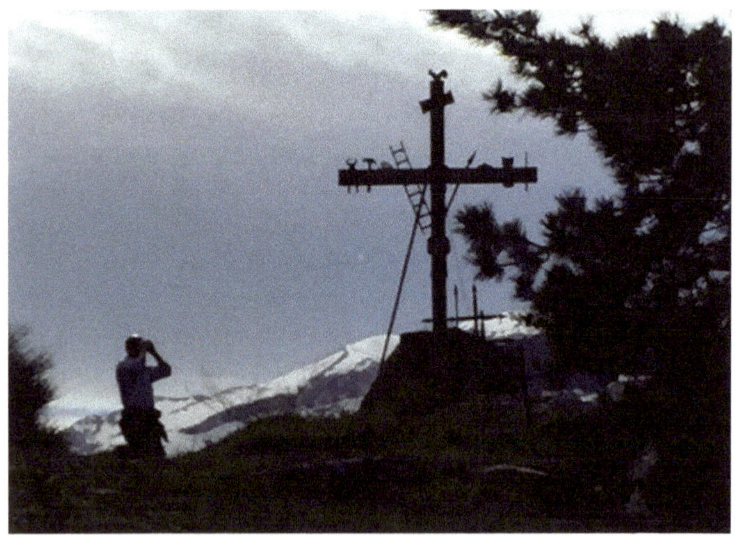

The Rev Dr Andrew Wakeham-Dawson

pointed out one in particular: "That's very rare." Unfortunate for that particular fly, Andrew ran out to the car and picked up his gear. On returning he promptly caught said fly in his net and had it potted in seconds in a bottle with some toxic-looking fumes in it. The owner was by this time looking nervous; maybe Greek Health and Safety had arrived and were going to shut him down.

Back to Italy and our eighteen-mile walk. It was not listed as that long, but certainly on the pedometer from the start we seemed to have clocked up 19 miles and about 2,500 feet, maybe 3,000 feet of ascent followed by descent. It was hard going, with an amazing fast-flowing river going down through the middle of the gorge. Much of the place had the feel of Yosemite National Park with enormous high cliffs and snow-clad mountains above. We reached a remote hermitage at the top of the valley having crossed three rickety bridges across the roaring torrent. At lunchtime, I did try to have a dip in a pool to the side of the torrent, having washed my face in it. It felt quite warm, but that was a fantasy; I got in up to my waist, and it was freezing cold. I did not get right under the water, because firstly I might have been swept away and secondly the rocks underneath were extremely sharp. The hermitage had a tiny altar that had been set up with a linen cloth on it and a cross made from two sticks held together with straw, similar to the one which we have sometimes put up as a family at St Blane's Chapel on the isle of Bute.

At the top of the valley, we crossed the Bridge of St Peter, which was above a very deep gorge, perhaps 200 feet long and only 15 feet wide at the most, down to the torrent below. Above us were high snow-clad mountains, and we were quite close to the snow line, although we didn't reach it as we had the day before. We had planned to continue on to what was supposed to be meadow land but realized that this would mean an even longer walk, so we headed down the other side of the gorge. In several places, the path was very narrow and at one point, along the side of the wall, there was a steel hawser to hang on to because the path was only about a foot wide with a drop of maybe forty feet into the roaring river below. We arrived back in town and headed for the nearest bar, where we seemed to upset the barman by messing up his routine. You were meant to take a seat and wait for him to serve you, not appear in the bar demanding loads of beer. The problem was made worse by the fact that his beers were in 0.2 litre glasses, and I for one needed at least three glasses to get rehydrated. We had taken three litres of water in the rucksack at the start of the day, but in fact we had drunk the whole lot when we were still an hour from the town, so it is fair to say that we were thirsty!

The plan for the next day was to arrive in Manoppello, the site of the Veil. We needed to find ourselves a room for the following night, so that we could arrive in Manoppello at a reasonable hour in the evening, having done a substantial-cross country walk as a grand finale to our pilgrimage. Our master plan of having walked across Abruzzo had not worked out because the area was much vaster than we had anticipated. We therefore would be collecting our car the following day for the final part of our trip to the Veil.

There is no doubting these walks are enormously focused on things to which we do not normally give much time. Andrew is a wonderful walking companion, able to identify many wildflowers and enormous numbers of species of butterflies, as well as other insects. We saw remarkably little fauna. We found some droppings and bit of fur from wild boar, but we did not actually see any. The only animal that we had been in touch with was the dog I described earlier.

We then asked the proprietor if we could leave our luggage, allowing us to have a day pack only, to retrieve it later, and she agreed. We decided that we would get a taxi up the hill to Decontra and then walk across to Manoppello. In fact, there were no taxis, so we ended up walking up to Decontra, probably about a 1,000-plus feet climb. Then we went up over the hills above that, so by the time we came down the hill to retrieve the car where we had first started three days earlier, we had actually completed eleven or twelve miles' walking over high hills again. We passed back by the Hermitage of St Bartholomew, and during our picnic at the side of the river, I managed to almost effect a cold immersion up to chest level before being too frightened again to go further in (what a wimp I am) just in case I got swept away in the torrent. I also had to leap about four feet, from one side of the torrent to the other. Somehow, leaping across a raging torrent where you know that if you slip that it will be your last manoeuvre seems to concentrate the mind somewhat. I jumped over with more confidence than when I had jumped two days earlier after my swim. However, this was a truly memorable picnic lunch of half a sandwich, some nuts and a Snickers bar, following a little swim below the Hermitage. In contrast to two days earlier, there wasn't a soul about and we had the whole place to ourselves.

On returning to our car and after much difficulty we arrived at the Regis Hotel. It was supposedly based in a pretty mountain village but in fact it was on the edge of an industrial estate at the bottom of the hill in a completely different place from that advertised. The town was called Scafa. We wasted a good hour trying to find the hotel, speaking multiple times to the lady in the hotel, whose English was not good enough to explain where they were. She seemed to be definitively against explaining they were in an industrial estate. Meanwhile our Italian was not really good enough to communicate exactly where we were to aid any description she might give us. However, remarkably, when we found it surrounded by garages and fast-food venues, we drove into a tree-lined approach and, sure enough, as the guidebook had described, we arrived at a very smart eighteenth-century villa with a nice restaurant where we had an excellent meal, with our first pizza of the trip. The guidebook had suggested it was near to Manoppello; in fact, it was quite a few miles from there, so it was just as well we had done this part of the journey by car!

At about 5.30 p.m., we departed by car for Manoppello. There, we parked and walked to the Basilica where the Veil, the purpose of our trip, was displayed. The Mandylion of Christ, St Veronica's cloth or the Cloth of Edessa, whichever name you wish to give it, is the centrepiece of the altar. The Basilica was very much as one would expect, given over to the veneration of this truly remarkable piece of cloth.

The evidence is that it is not painted, that it is extremely old, and as described earlier it was either given to Christ on his walk to Golgotha, when he wiped his face and the image appeared, or it could have been one of the burial clothes found in the tomb after his resurrection. Whichever, there is a sad, doleful face gazing out from it, which of course has formed the image for icons ever since. The church is laid out for vast hordes of pilgrims but that day hardly anyone was there. There were only four of us in the church. Behind the altar are steps up maybe to a height of 15 feet and down again to allow you to get close to the cloth, within a distance of eighteen inches. It is behind glass, and the layout allows you to have a proper look; it is also designed to allow pilgrims to pass by efficiently.

As such it could be regarded as the progenitor of all icons, which at least allows understanding of the term "not made by human hands". However, to me, its greatest significance is that the face is staring out at us with open eyes: the image is a resurrection image, not a pre-mortal one. This point is so startling that I had to read Paul Badde's book twice before grasping it!

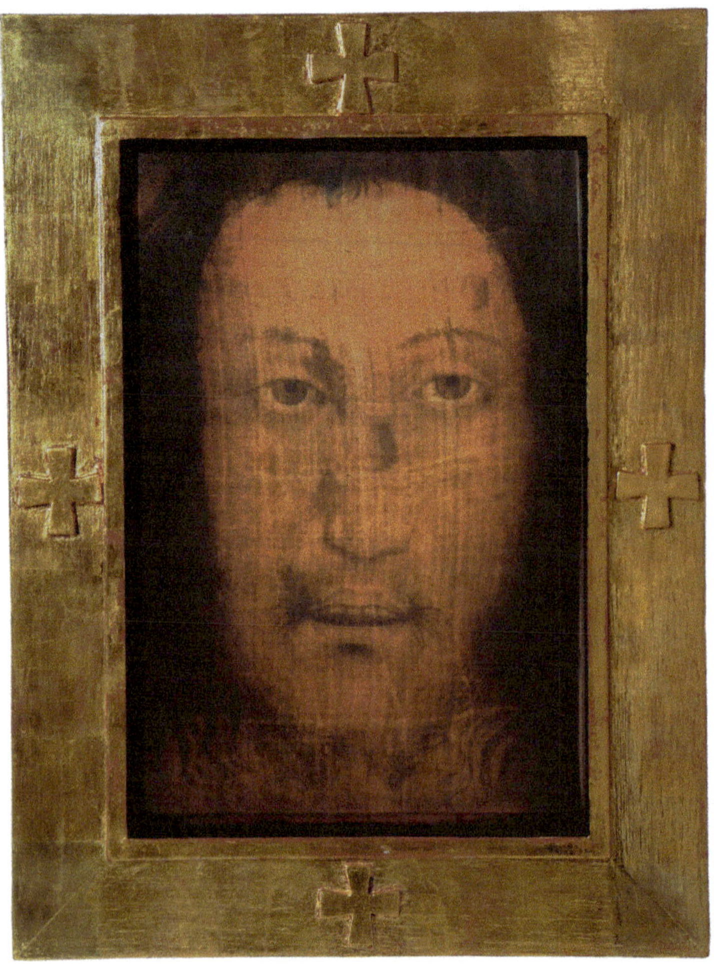

The Cloth of Edessa

The icon on page 57 shows Christ crucified on the wooden cross. His feet and hands are nailed to the cross. At his right side is the spear used to pierce his side, at his left the cloth soaked in vinegar which was given to him. Below his feet is a cave with a skull in it. This is Adam's skull with Christ's blood dripping on to it, part of the resurrection of man. The blood of Christ washing Adam's skull, the original man, leading to the saving of mankind. Interestingly, if you go to the Church of the Holy Sepulchre in Jerusalem, below the site of Golgotha within the church is a cave where Adam's skull is meant to have sat. When we visited a few years ago, this site was behind Perspex and the significance obscure to us. Returning to the crucifix, above Jesus crucified is Jesus within the Cloth, the Mandylion image again: this is the resurrected Christ, surrounded on each side by seraphs.

I have to say that I found it profoundly moving. I bought a few little things in the souvenir shop, including a copy of the Cloth, which was later framed back in London. We left and went to the town square of Manoppello, where we consumed a small beer and watched the menfolk sitting around smoking and drinking. The womenfolk all appeared to be in the church for Mass. We reckoned we counted fifty people coming out of the church, a number of nuns and in total two men. We never saw the priest appear!

We drove back down the hill to our hotel where we had dinner in the very unusual restaurant. It was all very smart, but there was a television beside each table, something neither Andrew nor I can bear at all, and we had our television switched off. It was difficult not to see scenes of Italian television whilst trying to engage in conversation. All in all this had been quite some trip, and tomorrow we were hoping to go to Monte Cassino.

Sadly though we did not get there, and our pilgrimage was over for another two to three years. Very splendid it had been. It was great to be able to talk to somebody like Andrew and to talk over matters spiritual, psychological, religious and professional for four days. All troubles had been forgotten and many of my ailments instantly better! The Veil, the progenitor of icons, had finally been tracked down to its mountain hideout.

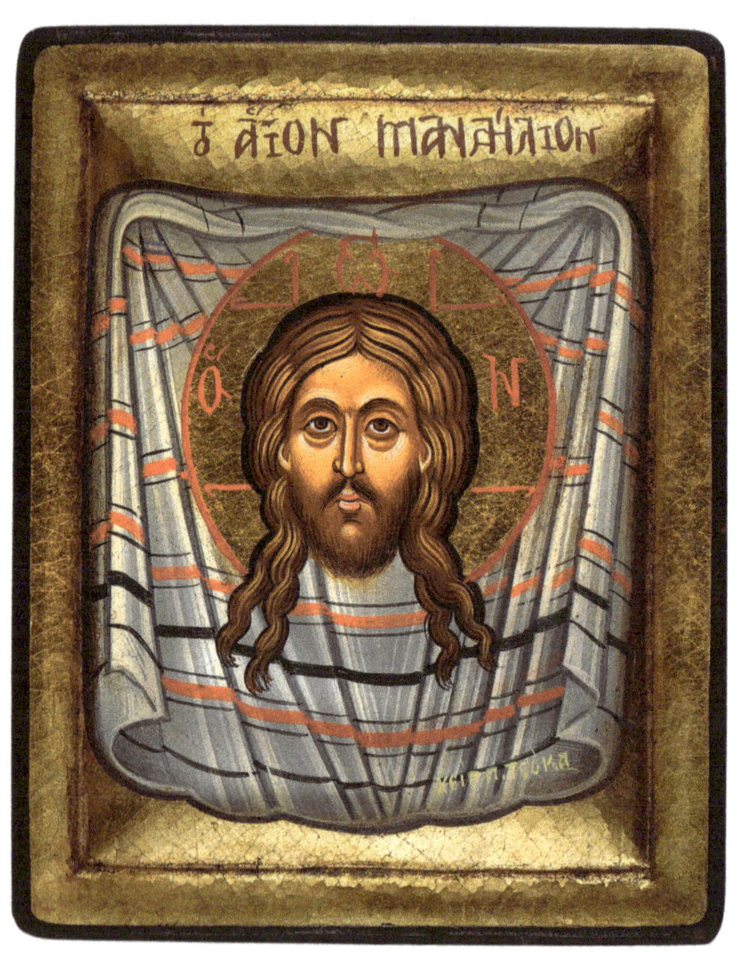

The Mandylion image

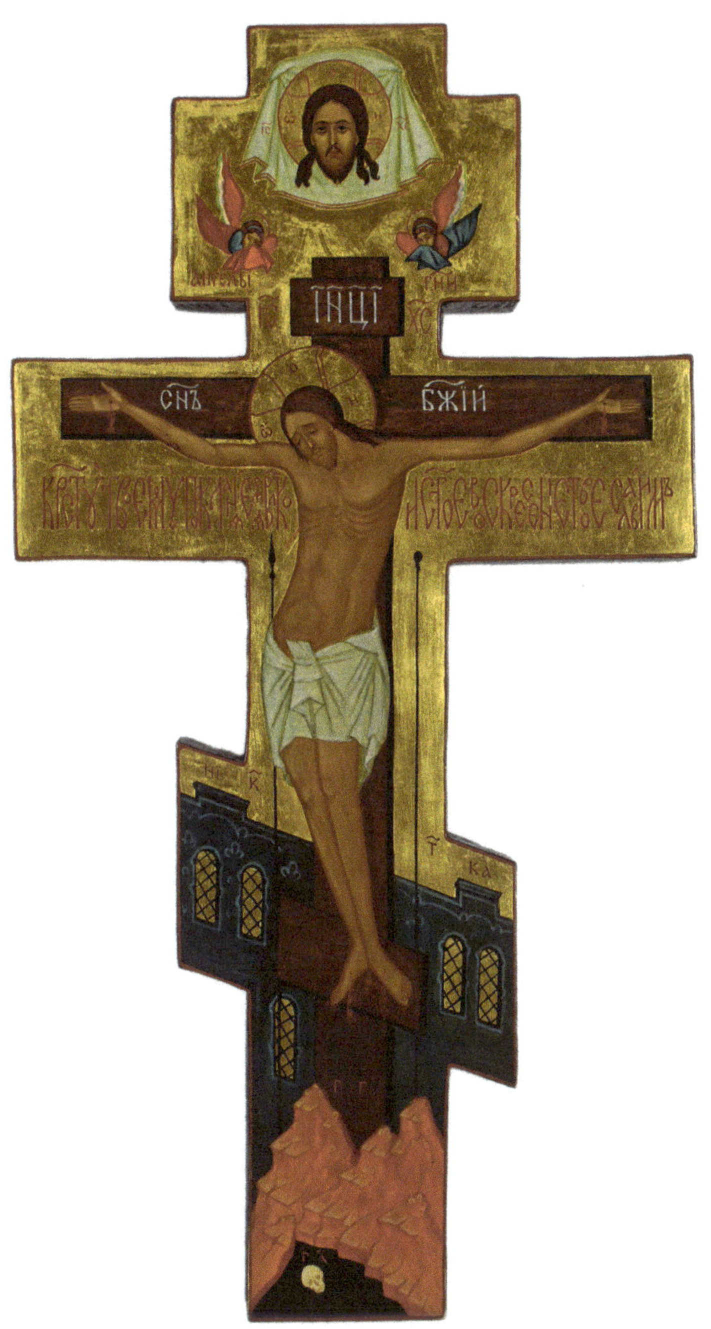

The Mandylion image on a crucifix

5

Cairo

Over the last few years, I have been fortunate enough to journey to the sites of many of the famous iconographic themes. This really helps to put the biblical stories into perspective. In my previous book, *The Journey* (Darton, Longman and Todd, 2016), I describe a visit to Bethlehem which for me proved uninspirational; it was my fault entirely for trying to pack too much into a short trip. The whole world knows that Bethlehem is the site of Christ's birth, and the icon that demonstrates the common use of caves as part of the symbolism has already been shown (page 16).

Following Jesus' birth in Bethlehem, Matthew's Gospel tells us that the Holy Family fled to Egypt to avoid Herod's slaughter of the newborn infants. I have to confess I have never given this part of the biblical story much heed or ever thought much of it. Matthew tries to present Jesus as the "New and Greater Moses", and therefore, as Moses' family in the book of Exodus lived in Egypt, the "new Moses" also has to go to Egypt.

In St Matthew's Gospel, an angel appears to Joseph in a dream telling him to take his wife and the young child and flee into Egypt. This Joseph duly does. This handily fulfils a prophecy, "Out of Egypt have I called my son" (Matthew 2:13–15). I suspect that this is where doubt as to the whole story arises. If you want to be disabused of this, you should visit modern Cairo where the Christian quarter feels very much like similar areas in Jerusalem.

I had the great good fortune to visit this fascinating city some time ago together with my friends Xiaomei, Hani and Diana to celebrate Hani's and my shared birthday on 15 January. We went to see the pyramids, the sites, the ancient artefacts, and we had much discussion about visiting a desert Coptic monastery. Hani's father, Gamal, had very kindly put some arrangements in place, but they proved hopelessly optimistic to fit into our timetable.

On 14 January, Xiaomei and I arrived in Cairo about 3 a.m. We had met in Heathrow and began our trip in a bar there, followed by a good meal on the plane. On arrival in Cairo, a fairly "hairy" half-hour ensued. We both had hand luggage only, but the car that was due to pick us up was not there; there seemed to be different banks of people with cards, but none for us. We looked at the rows on the inside and outside of Customs, and then decided to take a taxi. As we drove off, we saw a third line and later discovered that was where our man was hiding. Our driver had a somewhat mad style of navigating the traffic; we were subjected to a Lewis Hamilton style F1 grid getaway. It didn't get any better as we hit the motorway. Worse was to follow. In my mind we were heading for a Hilton hotel in the centre of Cairo and that had to be a minimum of thirty minutes away given the size of the city from the air. To my horror, ten minutes out of the airport, our driver careered across three lanes, shot through a gap in the central reservation, and then across the opposite carriageway's three lanes into a dark lane with no signs. Even worse, a bunch of men in dark clothing surrounded the car. I have to confess, my thoughts were, "This might just be my last trip ever; are we being kidnapped or are we about to be mugged or murdered?" Things were looking rough when the fellows opened the boot, looked under the car and then thankfully waved us on. We were at the back entrance to the Hilton Heliopolis, not the downtown one at all. We had just been inspected by security. What a relief!

The following day Hani and Diana had very kindly arranged for a driver called Wel and a guide, Amir, to take us around. This duo proved to be brilliant in every way. I have driven in many places but would not do so in Cairo unless I was in a ten-ton truck. I later learnt Cairo has the highest death rate on the roads of any capital city in the world. Most of the cars are dented; the city is vast and filled with tooting cars.

This a city which at least for me was a complete culture shock. Amir proved highly knowledgeable, which was very helpful over the next two days. Our hosts were returning from Aswan later in the day, so we would all dine together later. Our first day, 14 January, started with a trip to the pyramids. The drive across Cairo amply demonstrated its vastness. We arrived at the edge of the desert; this is walled off and the pyramid tops were visible in the distance. A negotiation then ensued as to whether we should use horses, camels or a carriage. Camels it was for Xiaomei and me, and a horse for Amir and the other two guides who were going to take us into the desert and round the pyramids. We decided to go for the full trip, which was not cheap, but absolutely brilliant and good value. The fellow running it cleverly didn't ask for our money upfront but let us take the trip first, so we felt much better about paying for it. It was a wonderful trip. We began by trotting through a very untidy area but then emerged through gates into pristine desert, not that I have much experience of deserts. The only similar thing I have seen was on the road between Jerusalem and Jericho, when I looked over towards Nablus and the desert there: the same place in which Jesus spent forty nights. The camel was comfortable enough, although I was high up, and it did spit and make quite a roar on occasion. Amir, who had a degree in archaeology and hailed from a medical family, had seemed somewhat reluctant to get on his horse. It transpired he raced camels but was no horseman; even I could see that by the way he sat. In fact, we swapped later on when it was obvious that he was in pain in a tender area! I'm not much of a horse rider myself but did pass a basic test in horse riding and stable management as a child and have occasionally tried it since. Many years ago, I had a girlfriend who was keen on hunting. I appeared in my old faun jodhpurs, bulging at the thighs and laced up at the calf, the First-World-War-field-marshal look; she almost died laughing. No hunting for me!

We rode up to a high escarpment which allowed us to take photos of the pyramids all in a line. I think there were seven, varying in size, with the Sphinx at the bottom of what was effectively a causeway down a valley leading from the Great Pyramid. We then trotted across towards the pyramids and dismounted from our camels and horses to start exploring. Inside a pyramid we climbed down to where the mummy had been entombed. It is handy to be of short stature on occasion, and this was one of them; Xiaomei is even shorter than I am, and so we both fitted down into the burial chamber reasonably well. We climbed out and visited one more pyramid before continuing downhill to the Sphinx.

It was at this point that Amir and I swapped horse and camel and we trotted/walked back across the desert into town. After the inevitable hard sell on souvenirs, we were driven back to our hotel, dusty and tired, but we had enjoyed a fabulous day. Later we met Hani and Diana for drinks and then went out for dinner, which was memorably taken in the Nobel prize winner Naguib Mahfouz's restaurant. We returned to the hotel after midnight and celebrated Hani's and my birthday with a stomach-settling crème de menthe.

Our second day, our birthdays, certainly put paid to any thoughts that the flight into Egypt was St Matthew's fantasy tale: what a revelation. Following breakfast, we were whisked by our wonderful driver down the now familiar route into town and this time to the Coptic Quarter. It is worth pointing out that I have never seen so many security forces in my life, it beats Israel hands down. There are multiple barracks surrounded by high walls with pill boxes and armed soldiers sitting in them, guns pointing outwards. Security was also high round the Coptic area, which was walled off and required you to go through security checks to enter it; it felt very like the Jerusalem experience passing from one quarter to another. We had now entered a large many-acre area with multiple churches. The first striking feature was the absence of litter and rubbish, the second the genuinely peaceful and tranquil feel to the place.

It is a very old part of the city based upon the original Roman settlement on the Nile, and the Hanging Church, regarded as the main church, has its base on the original tower of the Roman castle. This church is a truly remarkable structure. Coptic church design universally has a minimum of three chapels: a central one and two side chapels. The churches usually have twelve columns, although there is some variation on this theme. In the Hanging Church, one of the columns is encased after blood flowed from it when Egypt lost the 1967 Arab Israeli war. These sorts of phenomena sit uneasily with me as a scientist and surgeon.

The iconographic layout is different from the Eastern Orthodox Church: in fact, the Copts use the St Luke order of the New Testament, as I am in this book.

This made it relatively easy to take Xiaomei through the icons, showing the Annunciation, followed by the Nativity, the Presentation of Christ in the Temple, the Wedding at Cana, the Last Supper, the Transfiguration

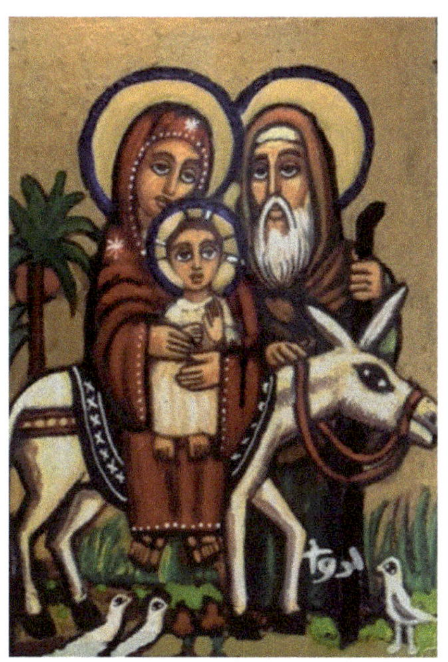

The Holy Family flees to Egypt

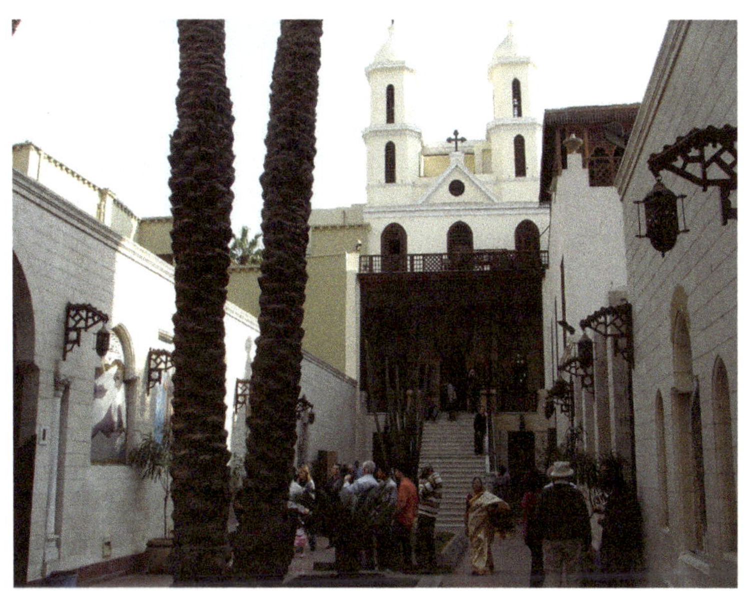

The Hanging Church in the Christian Quarter in Cairo

(wrong chronological order here!), Crucifixion, Christ being brought down from the Cross, Christ bringing Adam and Eve out from Hell, Christ in the Garden asking Mary Magdalene not to touch him, Christ Resurrected with the Disciples and doubting Thomas, then the Ascension and finally Pentecost. You can guess where our journey is going soon.

Following the Hanging Church, we ventured into the Church of St George, a Greek church restored around 1906. It had a splendid icon of St George slaying his dragon. St George's chains, used when he was tortured, were there to be touched in veneration. Also on display were a thoroughly unpleasant set of pliers, nails and other horrors. One can never cease to be shocked by the inhumanity human beings are capable of inflicting on one another.

Leaving this church, we passed between the Coptic and Greek churches down a passage where many good books were on sale. They reminded me that I had lost, happily now refound, my many books by David Roberts, the nineteenth-century Scottish adventurer and artist. We then entered the nunnery church of St Barbara, again laid out in a similar fashion with three chapels. The pulpits are all many-columned with a black one to represent Judas, a grey column for poor old Thomas, often maligned as "the doubter", and the other disciples represented in white marble.

The next church of Saints Sergius and Bacchus was the real surprise. It was consecrated in the fourth century and is the church where many Coptic patriarchs have been elected. It was built on the site where the Holy Family are reputed to have stayed. To emphasize the message, you walk down deep under the church to a small underground chapel in which is Jesus' stone cot. The stones from that time are kept under glass up in the main chapel. Also on many signs around the area is the Holy Family's route into, through and out of Egypt. They are reputed to have travelled to Upper Egypt and Joseph to have worked at the Roman Fortress. This is all very similar to the Jerusalem experience.

From the Coptic area, we emerged to have some light refreshment: Turkish coffee and a Sprite for me, Coca Cola for Hani, Xiaomei, Amir and Diana on tea; unfortunately Xiaomei's was served with curdled milk and needed replacing. Our driver then reappeared, as if by magic, and off we went to the Mohamed Ali Mosque, a vast Byzantine-type structure

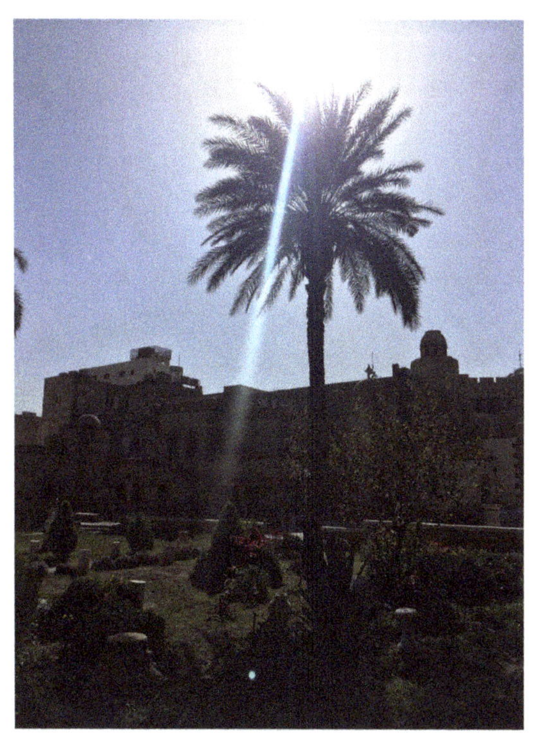

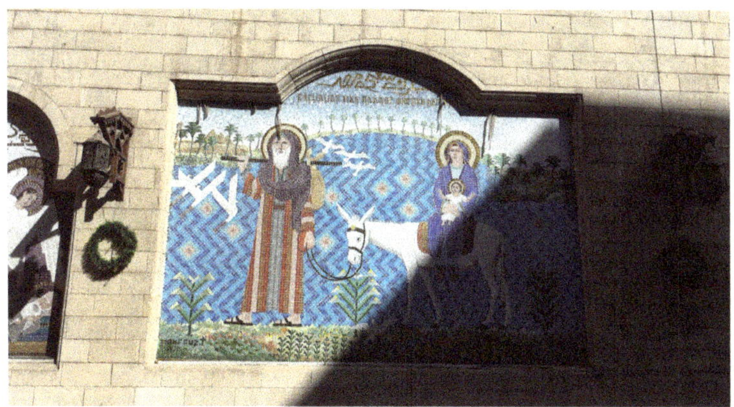

The Christian Quarter in Cairo

similar in architectural design to Hagia Sophia, as described earlier and similar in size to the Blue Mosque, also described earlier. We took our shoes off and walked from the courtyard inside to a beautiful building with much stained glass. On leaving we looked over the vastness of Cairo, with the pyramids visible in the distance through the haze. The Fortress of Saladin sits next door as well as a further palace where the French Empress stayed during the opening of the Suez Canal in 1869.

Our last day was memorable for a huge sandstorm; I had read about this phenomenon but with my limited desert experience had never seen one. I can promise you this type of storm does not exist in bonny Scotland. It was quite something: the sky turned to sand, the sun disappeared, the light dropped to dusk-like intensity, the temperature plummeted and, no surprises, the air was full of sand. It was time to go inside the museum to see the artefacts. What a great trip.

On the last night, late on over a nightcap, Hani, a great thinker and seeker of profound things, asked me, “How do you square up that Jesus died on the cross to mitigate our sins?” Now I have to confess, I had never given this any real thought until that moment; I also will confess I had no answer at that point. However, it played on my mind over the following months until Easter, when Xioamei and I were in the Anglican Cathedral in Athens on Easter Sunday. The thought came to me, and I have no idea whether this is in any way accepted thinking, but crucifixion and death in themselves were not the vital spark: I find it difficult to reconcile death on a cross with the expiation of our sins. However, it was resurrection which led to the disciples, all bar one, losing their lives to non-natural causes as they spread the radical teachings and new way of seeing life that were taught by Christ. This was the route to reduction of sin and saving us from our sins, as one tries to follow The Way, not sadly with anything remotely close to success, at least on my part.

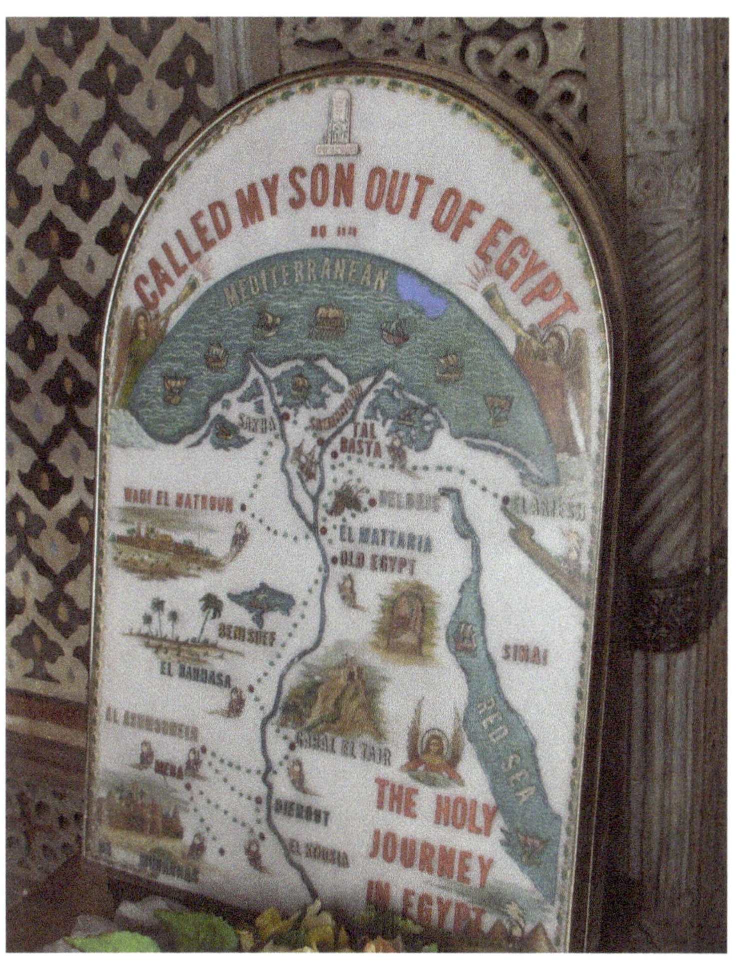

The Holy Family's travels in Egypt

6

Palestine: Jaffa, Nazareth, Mount Tabor, Yardenit, Galilee, Tiberius, Capernaum and Jerusalem

My next journey together with Andrew was by plane to Tel Aviv. We met in the Seafood Bar at Heathrow's Terminal 5 and caught up with each other's news.

After landing in Tel Aviv, we got into our hire car and drove to our hotel in Jaffa, the ancient city on the edge of modern Tel Aviv and the Mediterranean Sea. Late at night and tired, it felt alien and somewhat threatening; that later proved an illusion. The following morning, after an excellent breakfast where we followed tradition and removed provisions for a picnic lunch, we left in our hire car and went down to the port and fortress of old Jaffa, which was crusader country. We then headed north up the well-maintained motorway towards Nazareth. There was much building going on, a sign of prosperity, and the country was green and verdant.

It became clearer later that there is no fair division of water between Israeli and Palestinian. This water apartheid seems to me, perhaps simplistically, to be the root and possible solution to a lot of the Israeli/Palestinian conflict.

We had planned to visit the Church of the Annunciation in Nazareth, but on arrival found it very difficult to park. We were eager to get on with our hike, and Andrew and I, both scientists, though comfortable with Trinitarian theology and the resurrection from the dead, struggle somewhat with the virgin birth, so we decided to give it a miss, which in retrospect was regrettable. Much as I am dubious about the physical side, there is no doubt an underlying powerful spiritual message. There is a huge amount of beautiful Renaissance art depicting this event. In addition, my deep love of icons started with the icon of Mary conceiving Jesus via the Holy Spirit brought by the Archangel Gabriel, a very kind gift from Professor George Kourounis of Patmos University. He and his wife did me the honour of making their daughter, Maria, my godchild.

This ceremony took place in Athens and was an early, if uncomfortable introduction to the differing approaches to "crossing oneself". In the Orthodox tradition, one goes right to left, in the Roman and Anglo-Catholic (that's me) traditions, you go left to right. In the Presbyterian tradition, you don't cross yourself at all! In the middle of the christening, the priest declared me Catholic and therefore not qualified; happily, a domineering medical profession (there were many doctors in church that day) told him to "stop mithering and get on with it." He did, and I changed my "crossing" style to suit the moment; I have been versatile with respect to this ever since.

In the early 1990s, Professor Kouronis, and his and my fellow George Iatrakis, ironically took me from being an Hellenophile to an iconophile. This next icon was the one that properly started my collection. I already had St George and his dragon and St Nicholas on the sea, but here was a door to the New Testament, if not to a belief in Virgin birth, pretty appropriate in retrospect.

Luke 1:26–33

> In the sixth month of Elizabeth's pregnancy, God sent the angel Gabriel to Nazareth, a town in Galilee, to a virgin pledged to be married to a man named Joseph, a descendant of David. The virgin's name was Mary. The angel went to her and said, "Greetings, you who are highly favoured! The Lord is with you."
>
> Mary was greatly troubled at his words and wondered what kind of greeting this might be. But the angel said to her, "Do not be afraid, Mary; you have found favour with God. You will conceive and give birth to a son, and you are to call him Jesus. He will be great and will be called the Son of the Most High. The Lord God will give him the throne of his father David, and he will reign over Jacob's descendants forever; his kingdom will never end."

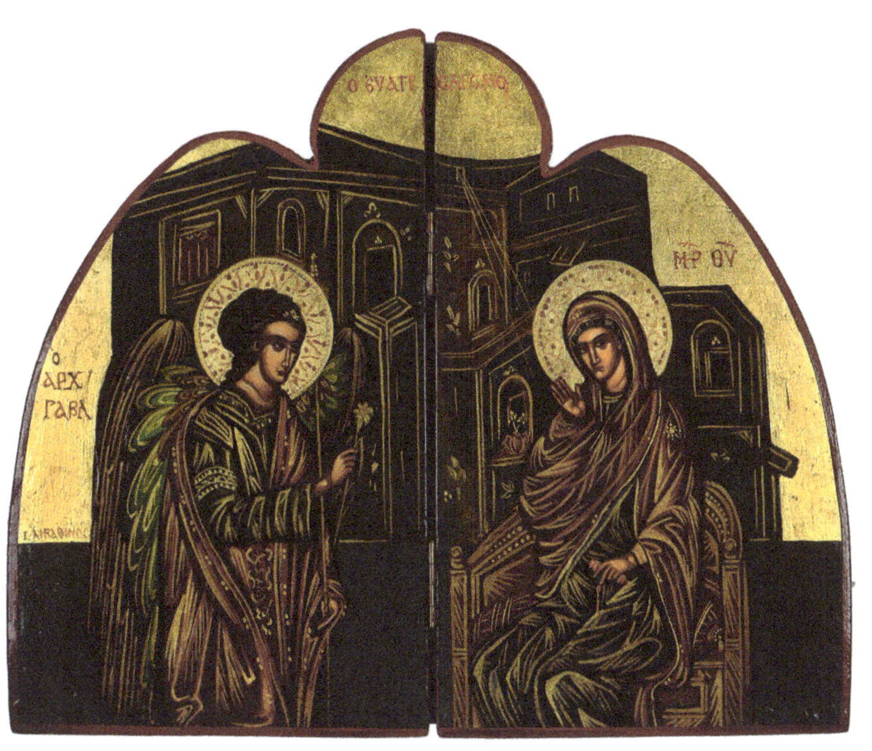

The Annunciation

After foregoing the church experience, we drove to a different side of Nazareth. It was non-Palestinian, with definitively new Israeli houses, and it felt very American. We parked the car, locked it, shouldered our backpacks and set off with the plan of walking over the hills to Mount Tabor. We needed to cross Mount Deborah. The climb was steep, rocky and much harder than it looked. The temperature at thirty degrees plus definitely didn't help. Mount Tabor remained in the distance, never seeming to get any closer.

Andrew and I discussed skirting Mount Deborah or climbing it; the former, we decided, was a wimpish approach, and not for us. To our enormous surprise, on gaining the summit we found a huge memorial statue, celebrating the silver wedding anniversary of the Queen and the Duke of Edinburgh, "planted by the Jewish Communities of Great Britain and Ireland" to quote the writing on the marble.

From there we descended into a Palestinian village, which seemed much poorer than its Israeli counterparts; there was much litter and detritus about. Andrew and I walked into the local store to some pretty amazed looks from the locals. Although we had set out with litres of water, we had drunk it all and proceeded to order litres of sweet drinks and water; we stood and consumed literally half a gallon of fluid each on the spot. The kids were impressed. The village was at the foot of Mount Tabor, the site of Christ's transfiguration. We walked out of town, sensing this was not a common sight, but, particularly after the mosque sounded for prayer, were treated with great courtesy by the locals, who set us on the right route. We then walked upwards in ever-decreasing spiral circles to attain the summit. There were many minibuses taking pilgrims and tourists up there, and it was such a walk that we were getting hand waves from drivers, particularly by the time they had passed us two to three times as we ascended. We arrived at the Franciscan monastery on the summit to find it closed, not just a little, but by hours. Andrew and I howled with laughter after all this exertion.

I have had a long-running obsession that this particular site was when Christ really came in to his own. I know that sounds strange, but this is when Peter, John and James really got to grips with who their leader was. They saw him in the company of the Prophets Moses and Elijah. The icon shows Christ centrally in a green Mandorla; on either side are Moses

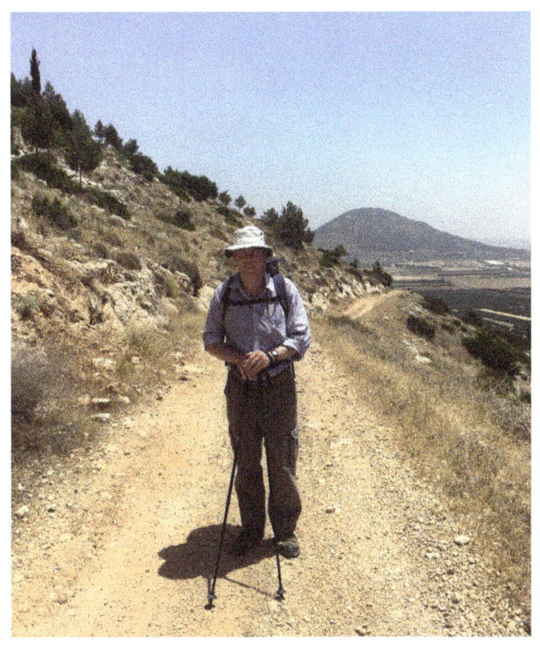

Andrew with Mount Tabor in the distance

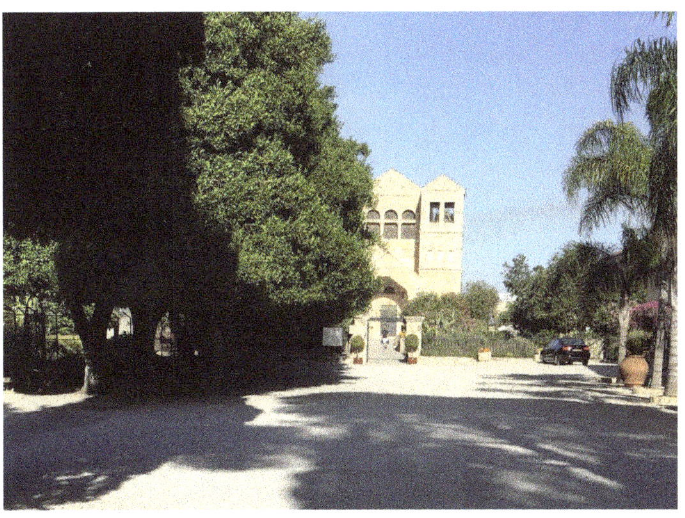

The summit of Mount Tabor

on his right and Elijah on the left. Prostrate on the ground are Peter to Jesus' right, John and James.

Luke 9:28–34

The Transfiguration

> About eight days after Jesus said this, he took Peter, John and James with him and went up onto a mountain to pray. As he was praying, the appearance of his face changed, and his clothes became as bright as a flash of lightning. Two men, Moses and Elijah, appeared in glorious splendour, talking with Jesus. They spoke about his departure, which he was about to bring to fulfilment at Jerusalem. Peter and his companions were very sleepy, but when they became fully awake, they saw his glory and the two men standing with him. As the men were leaving Jesus, Peter said to him, "Master, it is good for us to be here. Let us put up three shelters—one for you, one for Moses and one for Elijah." (He did not know what he was saying.)
>
> While he was speaking, a cloud appeared and covered them, and they were afraid as they entered the cloud. A voice came from the cloud, saying, "This is my Son, whom I have chosen; listen to him." When the voice had spoken, they found that Jesus was alone. The disciples kept this to themselves and did not tell anyone at that time what they had seen.

There was a huge piece of Jungian synchronicity a couple of months later when Hani and Diana organized for the same foursome who went to Egypt (the Gabras, Xiaomei and me) to travel to Lebanon, or the Lebanon as many know it.

This was a really memorable trip, but the synchronicity was our long drive to see the Cedars of Lebanon. Hani and I had expected a Scottish-style vast forest; not so. Since Roman times people have been cutting down these amazing trees.

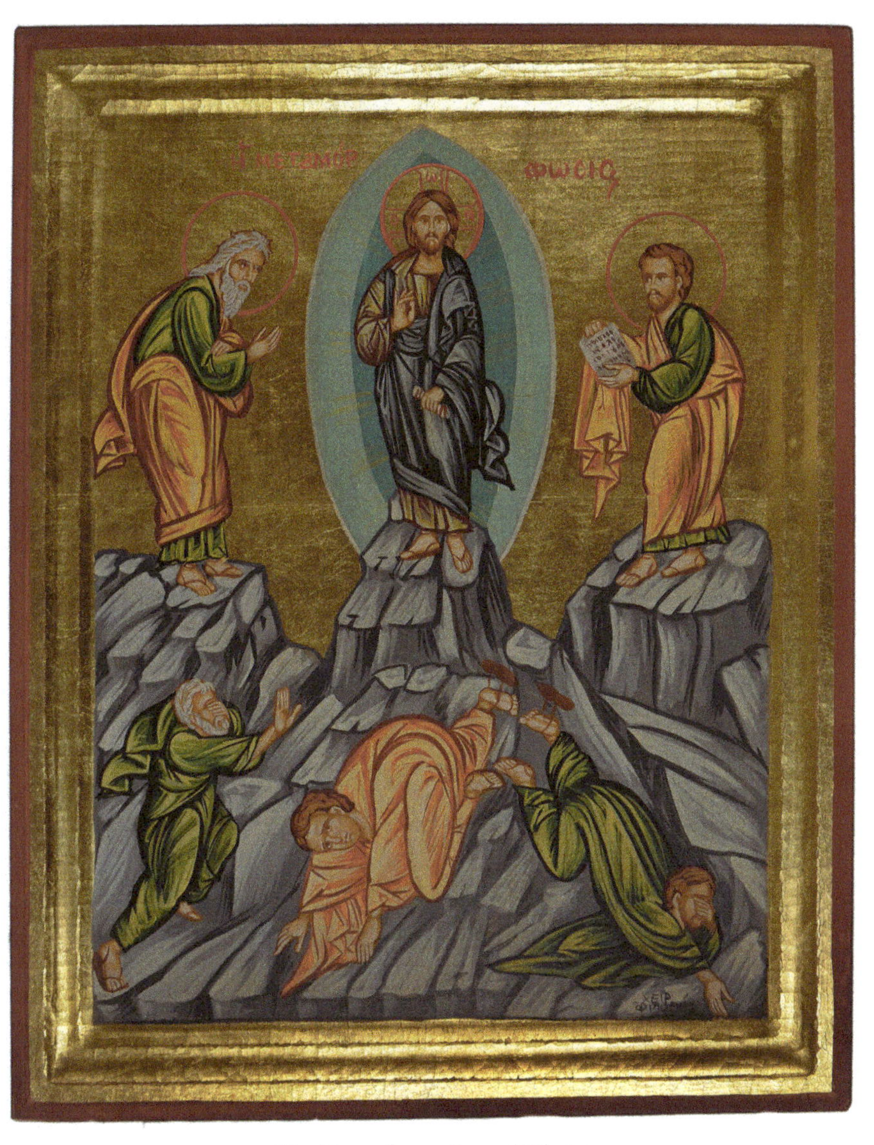

The Transfiguration of Christ

However, we had a beautiful walk up through the cedars and at the top found a church, the Church of the Transfiguration. This trip was transfiguring in many ways and taught me that through the disaster of my divorce I could survive, feel and love again; transfiguration is the name of the game. We did some tree hugging, literally, something I thought a few years ago was quite crazy; these days I firmly believe that trees have genuine souls. There are some that believe that groups of trees are protected by their own guardian angels; who knows? They have as much right as we do, I reckon.

Returning to our hike over Tabor: having turned up hours late we now had to descend, not a hard prospect, I know. However, unbelievably we became completely lost, going around in circles with nowhere booked to stay that night for good measure.

Just at the point when I thought I was going mad, we found a road and a romantic couple parking up. They walked over to the edge of the mountain and sat down to watch the sunset. Andrew looked at me, and we both knew we had found our way out. He suggested I should go and talk to them. I duly did and told them we were lost pilgrims. The woman asked me where we were staying. I had no clue but recognized that this needed sorting as soon as possible. She was keen to help, but her boyfriend reminded her they were up here for the romantic sunset experience. I didn't blame him; in a similar situation I would have been really annoyed too. I said, "Please enjoy the moment" and went off to find Andrew, and he and I duly hid behind a big rock to allow this couple their privacy, but still hoping to guarantee our exit from Mount Tabor. To further enhance your belief in our incompetence, we actually had a map, and also a 4G signal, so the internet map on our smartphones was working, but to no avail. We were lost.

However, the 4G contact and the conversation with the woman alerted me to the fact that we had better find somewhere to sleep and eat. In our minds, we had thought that by this time we would have crossed Tabor hours earlier and be en route to Galilee and finding somewhere to stay. The deal between me and Wakeham-Dawson has always been that we will sleep rough if needs be, and no whinging. Happily, so far this has never happened!

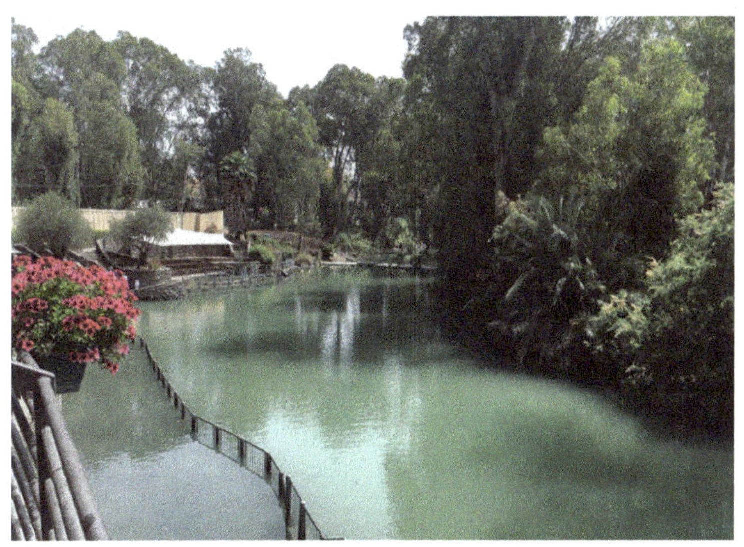

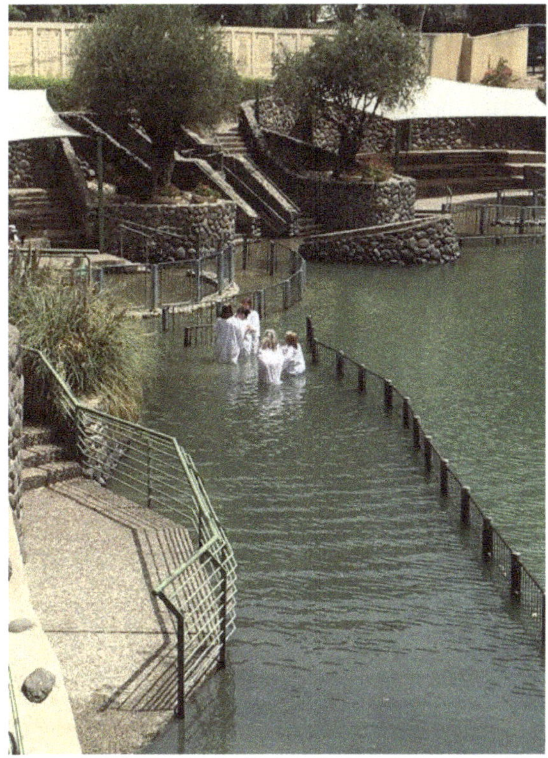

Yerdenit baptismal site on the river Jordan

By the time the couple's romantic moment was over, and using a combination of Google maps and an accommodation search I had found two places, one close, the other, a kibbutz, further away. I booked the latter, happily as it transpired. The couple in question proved to be real saviours: they drove us off the mountain and volunteered to take us to our kibbutz, but that was asking too much. Ironically, they took us to a petrol station opposite the first "Google" hotel, a dump, as my late father would have said!

They insisted on staying with us, and bought us all some soft drinks as they waited until the taxi they had called turned up. We discussed the merits of various types of hummus, a big subject across the Levant, I can assure you. They also really irritated the driver by insisting on a price before we got in. This young couple were seriously good adverts for Israeli youth, much like the young Palestinians we had met earlier; what a tragedy that two nations cannot share their beautiful country (and water) peacefully. I cannot help but quote Scotland's bard, Robert Burns:

> Then let us pray that come it may
> (As come it will for a' that)
> That Sense and Worth over all the earth
> Shall take the prize and all that!
> For all that, and all that,
> It is coming yet for all that,
> That man to man the world over
> Shall brothers be for all that.

Our irritated driver took us off to the kibbutz. This was acceptable, a Premier Inn type set-up, and we dined on heavy steaks in an American-style restaurant opposite. Much good conversation was had, although I suspected Andrew thought I was a bit of a basket case. Too true; he is an astute man.

Following a good night's sleep, we had a car take us back to Nazareth to find our own car. It seemed like days since we had left it but in fact it was literally twenty-four hours since we had parked up. We had experienced much which had revealed the apartheid nature of the country but also the common decency and generosity of both sides in this divided land.

Having collected our car, we drove, in maybe forty-five minutes, to Yardenit on the Jordan river. There are a number of these baptismal sites, on both sides of the River Jordan. There is no doubt that John the Baptist baptized in this area, probably at more than one site. A few years earlier, I had asked my priest and great friend Fr Gary if he would re-baptize me in the Jordan river. It is one of the few times I have seen him ruffled. He declared: "We are Anglicans not Anabaptists"; I backed off rapidly. Anyway, here we were on the Jordan and very beautiful it was.

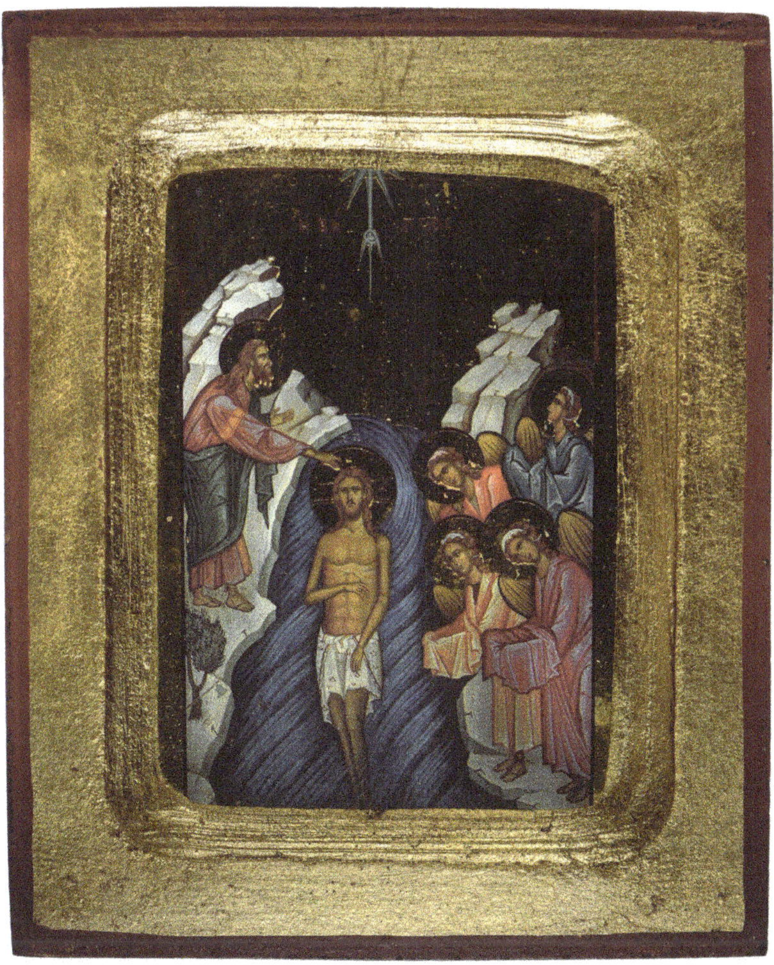

The Baptism of Christ

I'm a big outdoor swimmer—rivers, sea, pools, all are cool— but that day I just observed, soaked it all up and watched many devout people don white robes and immerse themselves in their various ceremonies. The whole deal here is that somewhere along this stretch of river Jesus was baptized by John the Baptist; now that is really something and worthy of many an icon.

The icon on page 79 shows Jesus surrounded by water, with the Baptist to the left, and angels to the right. The Holy Spirit descends from above, often shown in Renaissance art as a dove.

Luke 3:21–2

> When all the people were being baptized, Jesus was baptized too. And as he was praying, heaven was opened and the Holy Spirit descended on him in bodily form like a dove. And a voice came from heaven: "You are my Son, whom I love; with you I am well pleased."

The car was now parked, and we were off on our next hike, this time carrying six litres of water each. We set out from the Jordan river and soon arrived at the Sea of Galilee.

In both our minds we were getting into a short six-mile walk along the lakeside on the flat. However, the trail, as soon as we hit Galilee, led us uphill away from the lake. The heat was not conducive at 36 degrees Celsius. We both discussed that we didn't need to prove anything at this point in our lives, but of course, we did. So on we walked uphill by maybe a thousand feet to hit the higher trail, about the same height as the Golan Heights opposite. However, trouble set in: we ran out of water, and I for one felt very unwell. I was in front of Andrew and decided I needed to pee, only to find myself sweating heavily and peeing a few mls of dark brown urine. This I knew to be a bad thing (I'm a doctor after all) and this was pre-renal failure, the result of serious dehydration, which if not corrected leads to renal and multi-organ failure and death; this is what the SAS don't die of. They don't need to prove anything, but the reservists do. I had fallen into the trap of my own ego! By sheer luck about four hundred feet below us was an Israeli youth hostel, heavily fortified but certainly with plenty of water. I turned to Andrew and said, “I have to go there now, my friend.” I took off down the hill with Andrew in hot pursuit. We rang the bell and were granted access. We drank litres of water and soft drinks. I started sweating unbelievably heavily, which I had never done before, but happily half an hour later I felt normal and we continued our walk to Tiberius. When we arrived, we had covered over ten miles in high heat, with a lot of climbing, and needed food, drink and a rest.

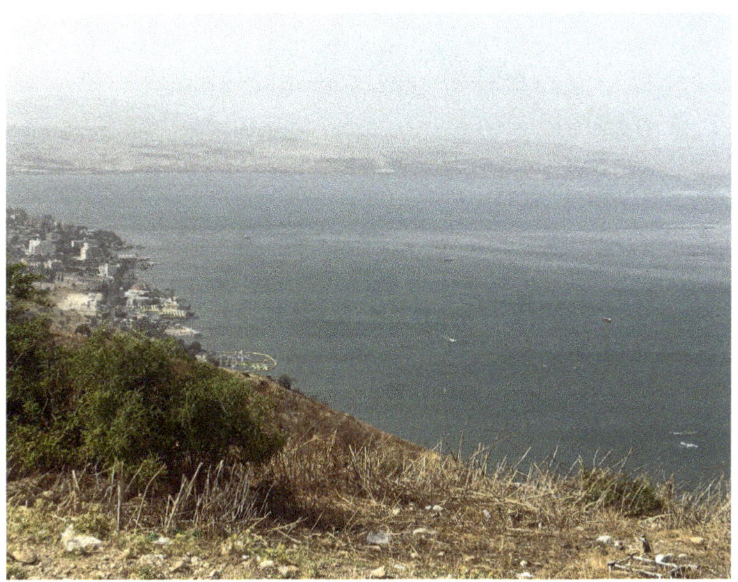

Tiberias and the Sea of Galilee

After leaving the life-saving youth hostel, we climbed back on to the high trail and came down into Tiberias. Google had found us a hotel, the Hotel Dona Casa, possibly the strangest hotel I have ever seen. It was a historic building with a huge galleried hall and a museum, but there were virtually no guests; it had a definite Hammer House of Horror feel to it. But our rooms were comfortable enough, so we washed and changed and headed out to wander about and find some dinner. Tiberias is built on the ancient Roman town, and this is obvious down on the shore. The modern town is in essence a lakeside tourist resort. We found our way to an area with many restaurants and finally, after a lakeside drink, we settled on a restaurant with a very welcoming waiter. During the meal, there were some loud explosions somewhere down the coast, maybe half a mile away, and the waiter joked that this was the latest missile attack from Syria. It is important to remember that Syria was actually less than ten miles away. The Golan Heights are opposite on the other side of the Sea of Galilee; just beyond that is Syria to the northeast and Jordan to the southeast, with Lebanon and Hezbollah to the north.

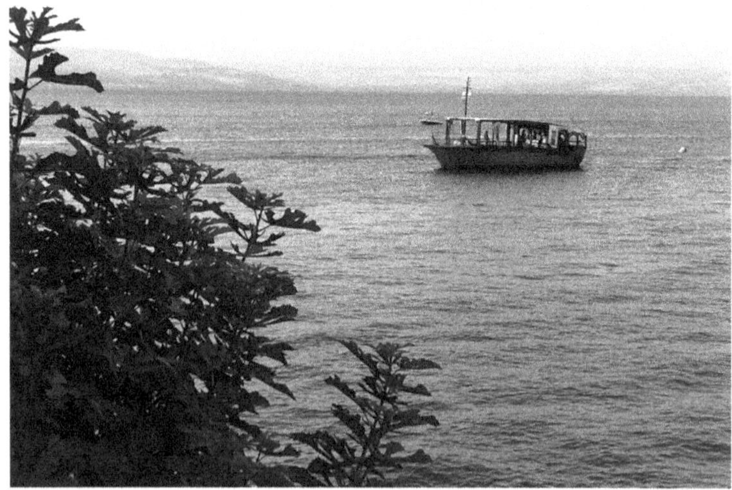

A pilgrim boat on the Sea of Galilee

We laughed since we knew there was a festival taking place with a firework display and told our waiter that we knew the real deal; we all laughed together. During the meal, we had a beer and a bottle of red wine which, surprisingly for myself and Andrew for that matter, we completely failed to finish.

Andrew in fact likes to water his red wine, not something I have been familiar with. Andrew explained that this custom came from ancient Greece and was something which Alexander the Great and his coterie would do. Anyway, for the first time in my life I watered my wine, and it was a big improvement. This stuff would have slain all comers. It was 14 or 15 per cent proof, and even watered we could not finish it. I was reminded of two things. First my late father would always look at the percentage. If less than 12 per cent, he would declare it harmless; if 14 per cent plus, it was going to produce a hangover and the vitamin B tablets would be produced which we all dutifully swallowed, I have no idea to what effect. Secondly I remember turning up at a dinner party exhausted on a Friday evening, when the host served Chateaux Musar, a very fine, but strong to the point of demonic, Lebanese wine. I fell asleep at the table during the main course. That was no wine; it was a general anaesthetic. The same applied to this particular wine in Galilee.

We returned to the Dona Casa Hotel, certainly a really spooky place. I have to confess I had my hunting knife on the bedside table along with my little travelling icon.

We departed this weird hotel the next morning. As we left, the security person on the front steps was toting a pistol. We took a taxi and went north a few miles up the coast, stopping below the Mount of Beatitudes, which proved to be a stunning site. We walked around the handsome church and then sat looking over where Jesus preached possibly his most famous sermon. The whole place was quite stunning. I cannot help but quote from Luke 6:20–38:

The Beatitudes

Looking at his disciples, he said:

"Blessed are you who are poor,
for yours is the kingdom of God.
Blessed are you who hunger now,
for you will be satisfied.
Blessed are you who weep now,
for you will laugh.
Blessed are you when people hate you,
when they exclude you and insult you
and reject your name as evil,
because of the Son of Man.

Rejoice in that day and leap for joy,
because great is your reward in heaven.
For that is how their ancestors treated the prophets.
But woe to you who are rich,
for you have already received your comfort.
Woe to you who are well fed now,
for you will go hungry.
Woe to you who laugh now,
for you will mourn and weep.
Woe to you when everyone speaks well of you,
for that is how their ancestors treated the false prophets.

But to you who are listening I say: Love your enemies, do good to those who hate you, bless those who curse you, pray for those who ill-treat you. If someone slaps you on one cheek, turn to them the other also. If someone takes your coat, do not withhold your shirt from them. Give to everyone who asks you, and if anyone takes what belongs to you, do not demand it back. Do to others as you would have them do to you.

"If you love those who love you, what credit is that to you? Even sinners love those who love them. And if you do good

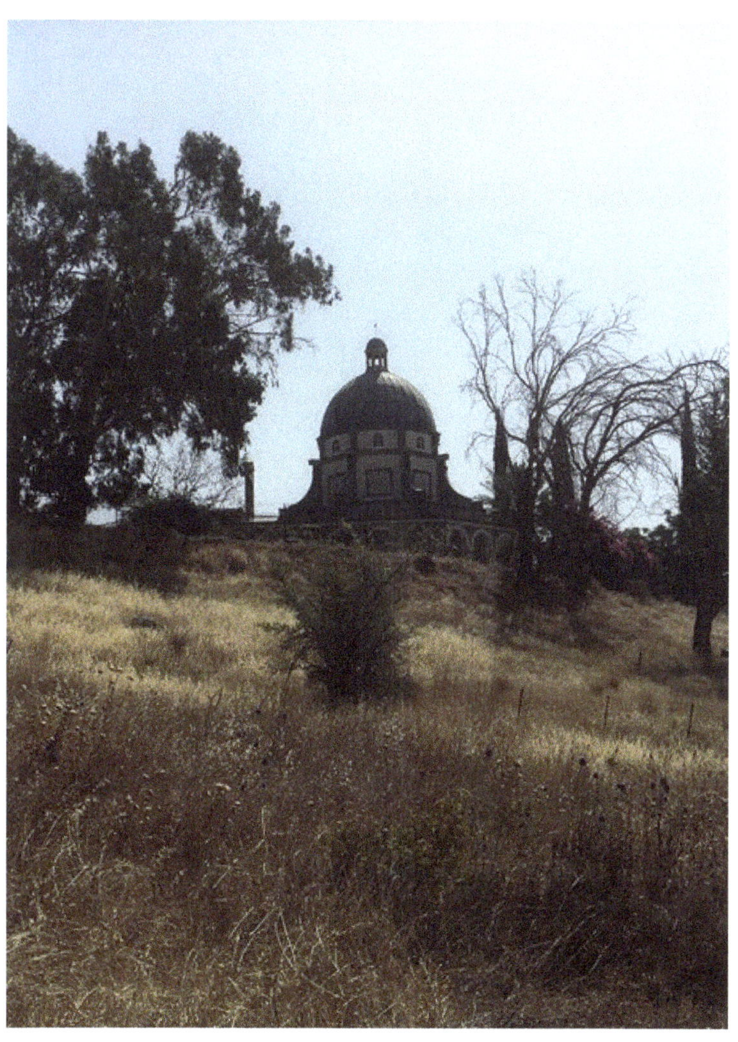

The Mount of Beatitudes

> to those who are good to you, what credit is that to you? Even sinners do that. And if you lend to those from whom you expect repayment, what credit is that to you? Even sinners lend to sinners, expecting to be repaid in full. But love your enemies, do good to them, and lend to them without expecting to get anything back. Then your reward will be great, and you will be children of the Most High, because he is kind to the ungrateful and wicked. Be merciful, just as your Father is merciful.
>
> "Do not judge, and you will not be judged. Do not condemn, and you will not be condemned. Forgive, and you will be forgiven. Give, and it will be given to you. A good measure, pressed down, shaken together and running over, will be poured into your lap. For with the measure you use, it will be measured to you."

We walked back down the hill to join a trail which goes by the name of the Gospel Trail. We turned left and walked up to Capernaum, saw St Peter's House, the Synagogue which was built just after Jesus' time, but almost certainly on the site of the previous synagogue where he preached. We saw statues of St Peter with the keys to the gate of heaven. The whole place was very moving notwithstanding the large numbers of pilgrims and tourists; but who are tourists and who are pilgrims?

That is a question!

We then walked down towards St Peter's Church, also known as the Church of St Peter's Primacy. I found this place right on the shore very beautiful, a really special prayerful place. There were huge numbers of pilgrims, many Germans and Russians, though no other Brits that we met. This place had further significance for Andrew, since his great-uncle had been stationed in Palestine during the Second World War and had written about this place in his diary.

Andrew is working on a book related to his own and his great-uncle's travels. I got chatting to a couple of tour guides. One was a Chilean who had been living in Jerusalem for the past twenty years, and he was with his brother and a couple of Swedish friends. We talked about the fact he had a Scottish friend who had done some walking in Palestine and liked hill walking. Another guide was an Israeli, a very charming man who we met again later in Jerusalem.

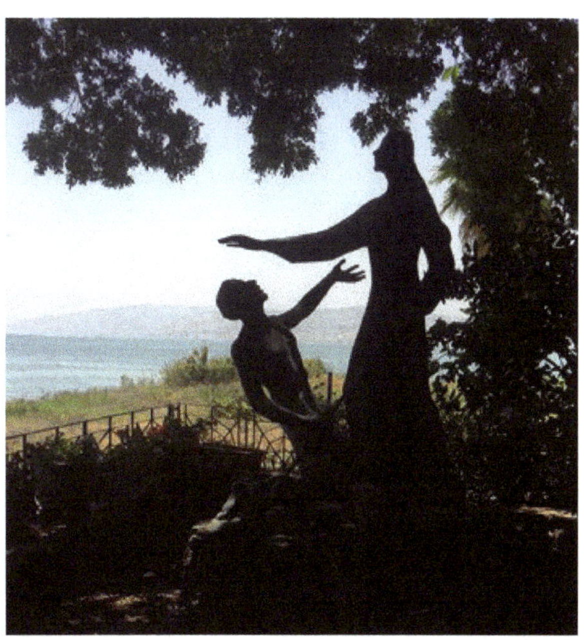

The Primacy of Peter with Galilee in the background

One of the things we had noticed and read about was that the level of the Sea of Galilee has dropped by five metres and is in danger of becoming a saltwater lake. This would certainly be a serious problem, since 60 per cent of all the fresh water for drinking purposes in Israel comes from the Sea of Galilee. I am no water engineer, but I am certain that they are either going to have to take less out or set up a desalination plant and put something in at the top end! As you look at all the piers, you can see how far the sea has dropped, and it was even obvious on the beach at the church.

We had decided to walk the Gospel Trail to Ginosar. To our horror the trail started to head away from the lakeside and up into the hills again; the temperature had not changed since the previous day and this exercise was to be avoided at all costs as far as we were concerned: no further attempts to kill ourselves with renal failure. We had the great idea that we would get right on to the lakeside and walk along there till we reached the museum in Ginosar. This contained what is known as the Jesus Boat. It was found in the 1986 excavation and was painstakingly dug up; it is 2,000 years old, and we were keen to see it.

Unfortunately we found ourselves in a real muddle. We followed a path down on to the lakeside which to begin with remained a path. However, it wasn't too long before it disappeared, and Andrew suggested we jump along the rocks and when necessary wade in the lake. This we duly did for over an hour. You would have thought, if you had seen us, that here were two fellows used to rock hopping on Scottish "beaches". You would have been right, but we were not in Scotland, we were in Israel and in its "hot" corner, a few miles from Lebanon and Hezbollah and Syria.

Andrew was wading in two feet of water, and there were many catfish about in the reeds. Now you know the problem: if you go the wrong route, the harder it is to admit it, turn around, go back and then take the right route. Here we were one and a half hours in and a large metal structure with lights on it appeared sticking out into the lake. If we turned around, it was an hour and a half back out, two hours on the trail over the hills in the heat and, to make matters worse, I reckoned that our destination was maybe a mile or two away. We were about to hit a three-to-four-hour detour, which was very painful to accept.

I turned around to Andrew, about a hundred yards behind me with his binoculars and butterfly net and hand signalled to him, back, or around this inconvenient structure?

Andrew waved his hand in the "go around" motion I climbed on to the structure, which was maybe eight to ten feet high, three feet wide and sticking about twenty-five feet into the lake.

I easily shimmied round, got slightly wet and then found myself in long reeds maybe eight feet high back on the shore. To my horror I looked up to see a high wall with barbed wire, pill boxes with gun slits and cameras. On a more positive note, about three hundred yards away was an elderly man with a van, and he seemed to be on my side of the security fencing. I thought, "If we can get to him, it will be OK." I moved through the reeds quietly and emerged about thirty yards from him. He took one look at me and started running for his van. I ran after him and as he reversed away, pretty rapidly I may say, I shouted, "Scottish pilgrim". He stopped and said "What?" I explained that I was lost and that I had a friend with me. At that point, Andrew emerged from the reeds wearing his little old beaten up white hat and clutching binoculars and butterfly net. What a duo! The old man, it transpired, had been in the merchant navy and had visited Glasgow; he knew that accent was genuine. He said: "Get in my van, while I make some phone calls" We complied, Andrew in the front and me in the back. Our new friend made a phone call, speaking in Hebrew. He hung up and asked us some more questions, then made another phone call and asked us more questions. After his third phone conversation, he turned around and said: "God sent me to save you pair today," and off we drove. I realized at this point that while we were starting on the right outer side of the security fence, the only road out led through the security compound. We drove along and passed through three checkpoints manned by armed soldiers with sub-machine guns and automatic rifles. They all waved; we were with the right man. He asked us, "Where are you heading for and where are you staying?" "The Jesus Boat and the kibbutz next door." The latter wasn't quite true as we had made no plans as to where to stay, but this did not seem the time to admit that. "I am going to take you all of the way there. No more walking today; no more getting lost." "Please, you don't need to go to the trouble." "Oh, yes I do," came the response, and he duly drove us to our kibbutz front door.

It was time for a sandwich and a drink. The kibbutz was much smarter than the previous one with a beach in front of it, allowing us to have a post-prandial swim in the Sea of Galilee. We left the kibbutz and wandered along to the museum where we learnt the story of the 2,000-year-old Jesus Boat and then saw it in all its glory.

We decided that we should follow the old man's advice of no more walking and that we should take one of the many pilgrim boats back to Tiberias. This proved harder than it looked. There were plenty of boats, but all were booked by groups of pilgrims; we needed to gatecrash a group. The pilgrim boat owners are missing a serious trick; they in fact only rent out to groups, though this is not wholly obvious. Even their website shows that boats go from Tiberias to Ginosar to Capernaum and then across the lake to the other side, from which you would think this was a bit like Windermere or a Swiss lake where you could just pick up a boat. In fact, you have to book them in advance. Happily we, ended up with a bunch of Romanians, who kindly let us on board as they hoisted their flag and sang their national anthem. Their priest gave a speech which lasted for about thirty minutes and made them all laugh a lot, but of course it was in Romanian, so we understood not one solitary word; however, it sounded as if he was a good speaker!

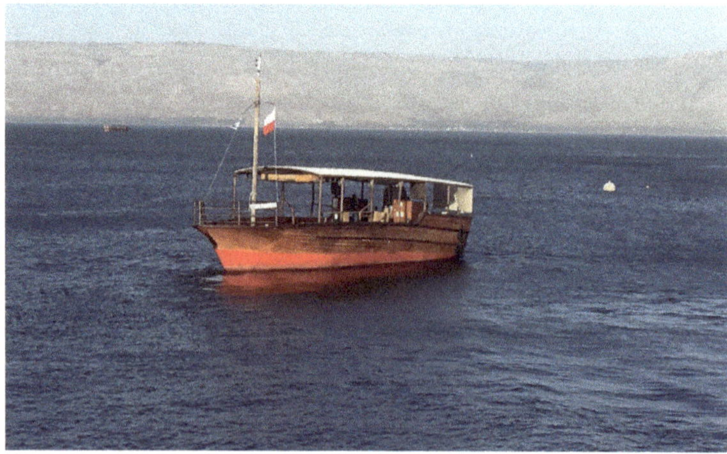

A pilgrim boat on the Sea of Galilee

Arriving back in Tiberias, we found a taxi to take us to our next kibbutz. We had decided we needed to retrieve our car, left at the baptismal site back on the Jordan river. The driver commented, "You fellows look like walkers, not taxi folks," which was true, but not today. We were quickly taken back down the lakeside and retrieved our car. We then drove to Kibbutz Kinneret. This enjoyed a splendid location; the rooms were comfortable and spotlessly clean. At dinner, I think there was one table of Evangelical Christians; Andrew and I, and everyone else were seriously Orthodox Christians.

This next morning we got up at 7.15 and met for breakfast at 7.30. The kibbutz had entirely changed its clientele; there were now hundreds of American college kids from somewhere in Florida, all with very few clothes on. The most amazing thing was they had been brought on a Jewish pilgrimage to visit holy sites; these boys and girls were going to have to find some clothes as they had no chance of entering holy sites in their current attire. I suddenly understood why my daughter Victoria used to walk around with so little clothing on; it was a national pastime and she was brought up part of the time in the USA. She and a friend appeared off the Philadelphia flight wearing tiny shorts and tee shirts. I was collecting them and saw all the drivers with their name boards looking at me as if I was a sleazo. The next thing, I had a plain clothes policeman on my shoulder asking me to come this way; they obviously thought that I really did look like a sex trafficker. A few questions asked and my driving licence and Victoria's passport showed the same surname. "Sorry for disturbing you sir, have a safe journey," concluded the episode.

After a fairly unexciting breakfast, we then got in the car and drove back to Jaffa to our hotel, which we had not liked the first time, but I have to say that we had misjudged it, and it seemed quite nice second time around. It is always difficult arriving somewhere at 2 a.m. The area which we had perceived as a bit of a slum really wasn't at all, it was decent. The tired mind plays tricks, particularly when you arrive somewhere unknown. We had returned to Jaffa to collect our suitcases. We had not felt happy to leave them in the car, and for our hiking we carried few clothes.

Then we were on the road to Jerusalem. It was a bit difficult getting out of Tel Aviv, but we found our way and when we got to Jerusalem, I remembered it quite well, and we arrived at the American Colony Hotel without a hitch; no repeat of the last *Bonfire of the Vanities* experience. Andrew and I shared a sandwich in the beautiful courtyard of our hotel and then went around the corner to St George's Cathedral to take some photos at the same site that his great-uncle had photographed. Andrew sent a message to the Dean, but we did not see him. We then passed by the Garden Tomb; it is very beautiful and gives a complete sense of what a tomb in Jesus' time was like, even if this is not the actual tomb.

We then passed through the ancient walls of medieval Jerusalem on to the Via Dolorosa. This transit of the city walls seems the appropriate place to bring in Christ entering Jerusalem on Palm Sunday, although we had just encountered the medieval walls, not the Roman ones that Jesus would have known.

The icon on page 93 shows Christ on the colt, with children placing clothes and palms at his feet. The disciples are behind him and the city and its people in front of him. Behind is a hill and a tree representing Golgotha. There is also a small child in the tree.

Luke 19:28–38

After Jesus had said this, he went on ahead, going up to Jerusalem. As he approached Bethphage and Bethany at the hill called the Mount of Olives, he sent two of his disciples, saying to them, "Go to the village ahead of you, and as you enter it, you will find a colt tied there, which no one has ever ridden. Untie it and bring it here. If anyone asks you, 'Why are you untying it?' say, 'The Lord needs it.'"

Those who were sent ahead went and found it just as he had told them. As they were untying the colt, its owners asked them, "Why are you untying the colt?"

They replied, "The Lord needs it."

They brought it to Jesus, threw their cloaks on the colt and put Jesus on it. As he went along, people spread their cloaks on the road.

When he came near the place where the road goes down the Mount of Olives, the whole crowd of disciples began joyfully to praise God in loud voices for all the miracles they had seen:

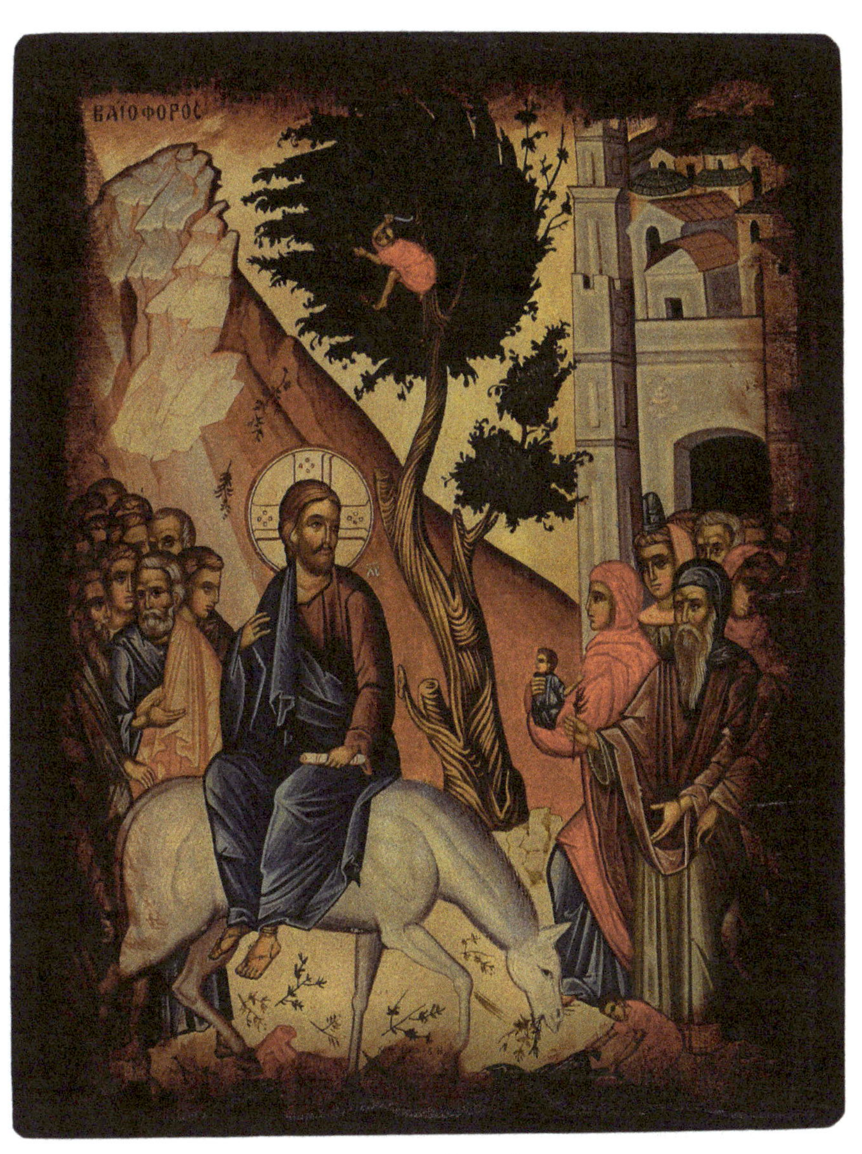

Christ enters Jerusalem

> "Blessed is the king who comes in the name of the Lord!"
> "Peace in heaven and glory in the highest!"

Returning to the Via Dolorosa, I described this walk in detail in my previous book, *The Journey.* This time some stations were shut which were open the last time and vice versa. We duly arrived at the Church of the Holy Sepulchre. What an amazing place! I understood the Church much better this time. There were various services going on, and this time we were able to go into the Holy Sepulchre chapel itself. This is the same chapel that the Patriarch emerges from at Easter with the Jerusalem fire.

We visited the Armenian one at the back as well. The inside of the tomb is profoundly moving. There are no more than three people in the chapel at any one time and you kneel with your head on the slab—more on this later. At first, we were unable to ascend the stairs to the "Golgotha level", the site of crucifixion, because there was a service in progress, but in fact the ladder that was put to block the way was removed and we were all allowed up to take part in the Franciscan service, which was sung in Latin and was very beautiful.

From there, we came down to the Stone of Lamentation, and the whole layout of the church with its many levels really makes sense. In the Bible story, Christ is crucified on the hill of Golgotha, a high rock, so that the populace could see the punishment which was being inflicted. The church is built right over the top of this rocky hill, so you do really climb to Golgotha whilst within the church. The Stone of Lamentation lies below the hill; this is what one would expect. It should lie close to the foot of the hill, as Christ was removed from the Cross and placed directly on to the stone. Within the church it lies close to the entrance, directly below Golgotha. The Holy Sepulchre, the tomb where Jesus was buried and emerged from lies close by, probably a hundred feet or so, and of course this is also contained within the main church; it's all under one roof. The cloths were in this tomb, the garden Christ emerged into was here, within the church or very nearby, where he told Mary Magdalene "Touch me not." This seems the right time to connect with two of our icons, Crucifixion and Mary Magdalene in the garden.

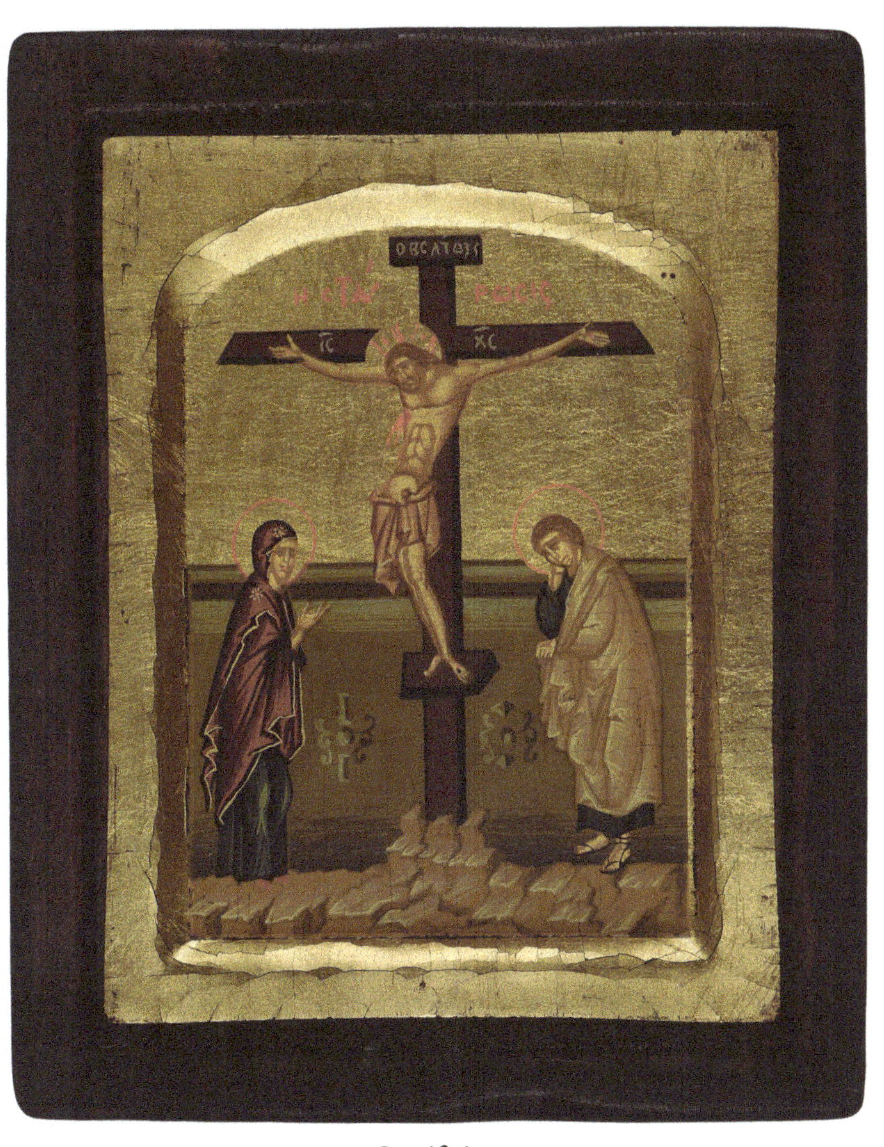

Crucifixion

The icon on page 95 shows Christ crucified with Mary the Mother of God to Jesus' right and John, the beloved disciple, to the left. Above the cross are the initials in Greek, the equivalent of the Latin INRI, which translates as Jesu Nazarene, Rex (King), Judea.

Luke 23:20–49

Wanting to release Jesus, Pilate appealed to them again. But they kept shouting, "Crucify him! Crucify him!"

For the third time he spoke to them: "Why? What crime has this man committed? I have found in him no grounds for the death penalty. Therefore I will have him punished and then release him."

But with loud shouts they insistently demanded that he be crucified, and their shouts prevailed. So Pilate decided to grant their demand. He released the man who had been thrown into prison for insurrection and murder, the one they asked for, and surrendered Jesus to their will.

As the soldiers led him away, they seized Simon from Cyrene, who was on his way in from the country, and put the cross on him and made him carry it behind Jesus. A large number of people followed him, including women who mourned and wailed for him. Jesus turned and said to them, "Daughters of Jerusalem, do not weep for me; weep for yourselves and for your children. For the time will come when you will say, 'Blessed are the childless women, the wombs that never bore and the breasts that never nursed!'

Then "'they will say to the mountains, "Fall on us!" and to the hills, "Cover us!"'

For if people do these things when the tree is green, what will happen when it is dry?"

Two other men, both criminals, were also led out with him to be executed. When they came to the place called the Skull, they crucified him there, along with the criminals—one on his right, the other on his left. Jesus said, "Father, forgive them, for they do not know what they are doing." And they divided up his clothes by casting lots.

The people stood watching, and the rulers even sneered at him. They said, "He saved others; let him save himself if he is God's Messiah, the Chosen One."

The soldiers also came up and mocked him. They offered him wine vinegar and said, "If you are the king of the Jews, save yourself."

There was a written notice above him, which read: THIS IS THE KING OF THE JEWS.

One of the criminals who hung there hurled insults at him: "Aren't you the Messiah? Save yourself and us!"

But the other criminal rebuked him. "Don't you fear God," he said, "since you are under the same sentence? We are punished justly, for we are getting what our deeds deserve. But this man has done nothing wrong."

Then he said, "Jesus, remember me when you come into your kingdom."

Jesus answered him,"Truly I tell you, today you will be with me in paradise."

The Death of Jesus

It was now about noon, and darkness came over the whole land until three in the afternoon, for the sun stopped shining. And the curtain of the temple was torn in two. Jesus called out with a loud voice, "Father, into your hands I commit my spirit." When he had said this, he breathed his last.

The centurion, seeing what had happened, praised God and said, "Surely this was a righteous man." When all the people who had gathered to witness this sight saw what took place, they beat their breasts and went away. But all those who knew him, including the women who had followed him from Galilee, stood at a distance, watching these things.

At this juncture to maintain our chronology The Cloth should be looked at again and the detail observed. This is the vital part of the story from crucifixion to resurrection.

Luke 24:12

> Peter, however, got up and ran to the tomb. Bending over, he saw the strips of linen lying by themselves, and he went away, wondering to himself what had happened.

The first person to see the risen Christ is Mary Magdalene.

This is a complex icon, which shows Mary Magdalene at the tomb (page 99). Also in the background is Lazarus bound in funeral linen clothes and, of course, Jesus as a baby swaddled. Also, in the far background Golgotha can be seen.

Unfortunately, St Luke doesn't cover this theme, except briefly.

Luke 24:9–11

> When they came back from the tomb, they told all these things to the Eleven and to all the others. It was Mary Magdalene, Joanna, Mary the mother of James, and the others with them who told this to the apostles. But they did not believe the women, because their words seemed to them like nonsense.

However, John's Gospel is more fulsome and in the vein of the iconographic image.

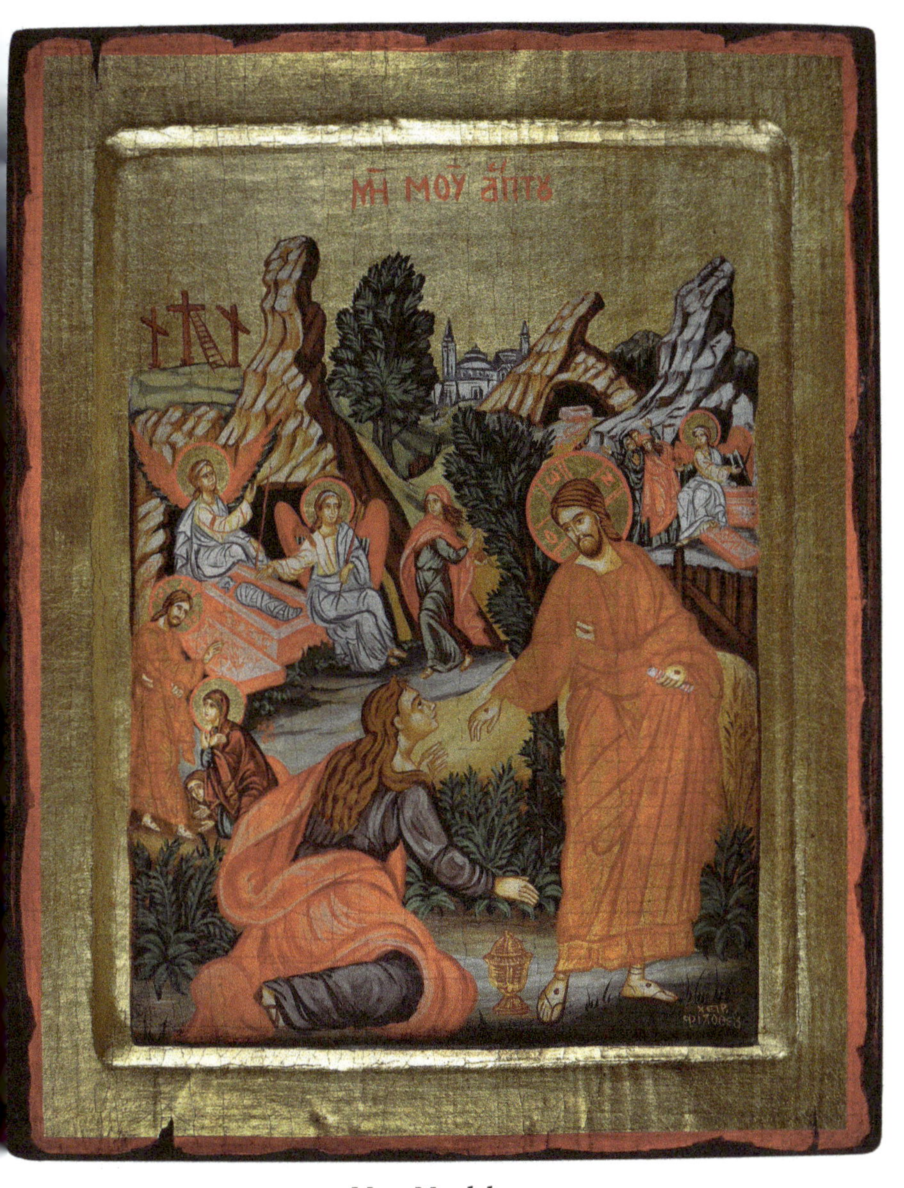

Mary Magdalene

John 20:11–17

> Now Mary stood outside the tomb crying. As she wept, she bent over to look into the tomb and saw two angels in white, seated where Jesus' body had been, one at the head and the other at the foot.
>
> They asked her, "Woman, why are you crying?"
>
> "They have taken my Lord away," she said, "and I don't know where they have put him." At this, she turned around and saw Jesus standing there, but she did not realize that it was Jesus.
>
> He asked her, "Woman, why are you crying? Who is it you are looking for?"
>
> Thinking he was the gardener, she said, "Sir, if you have carried him away, tell me where you have put him, and I will get him."
>
> Jesus said to her, "Mary."
>
> She turned toward him and cried out in Aramaic, "Rabboni!" (which means "Teacher").
>
> Jesus said, "Do not hold on to me, for I have not yet ascended to the Father. Go instead to my brothers and tell them, 'I am ascending to my Father and your Father, to my God and your God.'"

That evening we ate at our hotel, and very lovely it was. I didn't sleep so well; as for dinner I had hummus and lamb followed by some stuffed vine leaves. I am not sure which component of all that I had eaten that day contributed, but I certainly had some gastrointestinal problems which stopped me from sleeping as well as I might. In addition, we had seen so much, so much to take in.

Certainly, I have no doubt that the Church of the Holy Sepulchre ticks all the boxes for the geographical site of this plethora of iconographic images. I had also found myself profoundly moved when I, for the first time, had placed my head on Christ's tomb; here, as the Celts would say, was a seriously "thin place". In fact, in truth it felt like a bolt passing right through my head followed by a great feeling of joy, contentment, love and forgiveness. The hidden door had opened; here was that wonderful

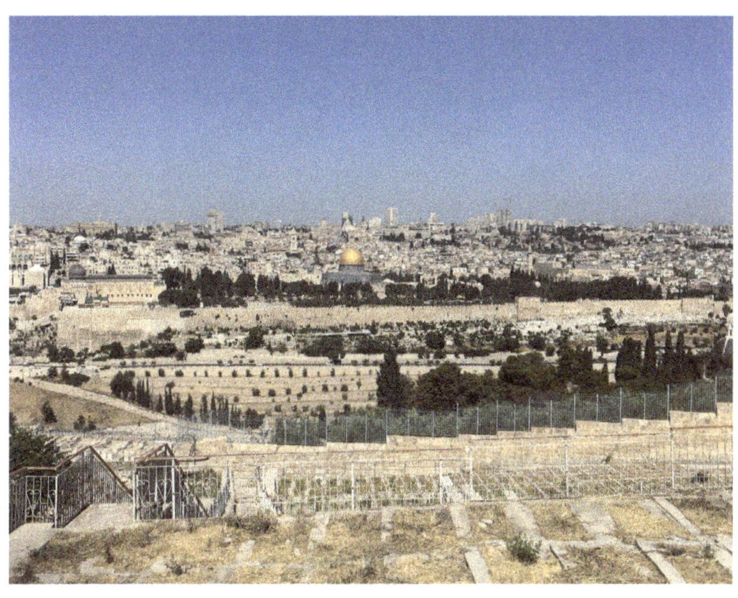

Jerusalem from the Mount of Olives

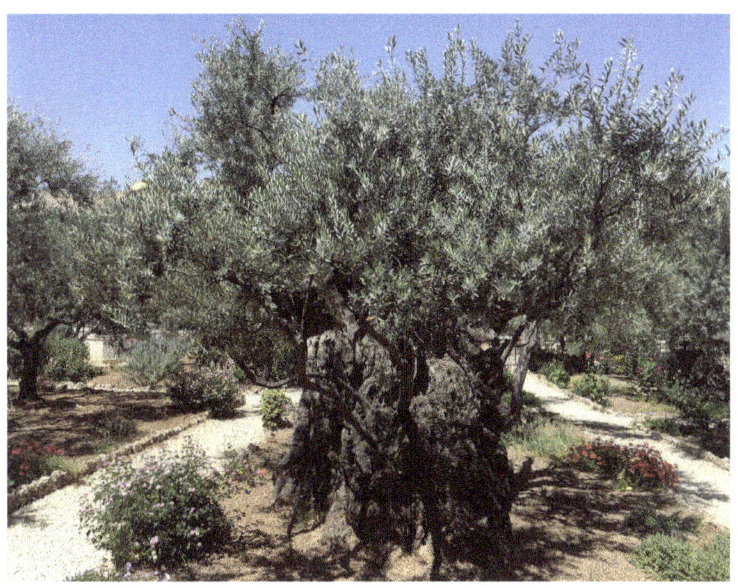

The Garden of Gethsemane

rare event so worth seeking and so elusive. I experienced something similar at the tomb of St Margaret in Dunfermline Abbey many years ago. The Reformation in 1559 might have destroyed her Reliquary Chapel, but they had failed to dissipate the healing energies which still come from the blocks of Frosterley "marble" which formed the original base. Somehow that day in Jerusalem, at that moment, I gained insights into my life that had previously escaped me.

The following morning after breakfast we found Mosa, who drove us around five years ago, to take us once again up to the Mount of Olives. This time we visited the Chapel of the Ascension on Mount Carmel and then went down on to the Mount of Olives where we took in the amazing view. We then wandered down to the Church of Dominus Flevit—such a beautiful place—and were fortunate to go in with a French group, who had their priest with them. We took Mass with them. They were very welcoming, and Andrew and I speak enough French to follow the service; it is easy if you are Catholic anyway. We then went outside; I looked for the site of the burial of the third Marquis of Bute's heart, which is sadly unmarked. The third Marquis of Bute was terrified of being buried alive and was also a fervent Scottish Nationalist; following Robert the Bruce's lead, after he died, he had his heart cut out and taken to Jerusalem, where it was buried in the grounds of Dominus Flevit.

The silver casket was returned to Mount Stuart House, the family seat on Bute. Robert the Bruce's heart was taken to Jerusalem by his old friend and fighting companion the Black Douglas.

We wandered down the hill past the Russian Orthodox Church of St Mary Magdalene, which was closed, as it had been the previous time I tried to visit, although this time we spied a couple of nuns who went into the convent. The Garden of Gethsemane lay below us and to the left, with its ancient olive trees and great beauty.

For many years I had wanted to see the Pool of Siloam. My late father introduced me to a beautiful hymn sung by the Glasgow Orpheus Choir conducted by Sir Hugh Robertson. Dad had met him as a young man in the 1940s. The hymn starts with the line "By cool Siloam's shady rill".

The other famous pool in Jerusalem is that of Bethesda, which I hadn't seen either. Both are associated with healing properties at Jesus' hands. From the Kidron Valley, as you approach it descending the Mount of

Olives, we walked up the hill to the right looking for the Pool of Siloam, but in fact we had gone in completely the wrong direction; we should have gone left. We came back along to the Lions' Gate through a fairly squalid tip site and then entered Jerusalem and walked through the medieval city to the Western Wall. As we were walking through Old Jerusalem, we attempted to gain access to the area around the Dome of the Rock.

At the time of my previous visit, the Dome of the Rock mosque itself was shut; this time the entire Muslim platform was closed and some fairly brusque guards told us we were not Muslim and therefore we were not going in. An even bigger home goal, I am afraid, than the last time. It was interesting because the contrast at the Western Wall was enormous; there were many people there to welcome you even if you were not Jewish. I certainly was given a prayer slip on which I wrote a very short prayer for my family. When I approached the Western Wall, I did as all the Jewish people do and inserted the prayer into the wall. It was very moving. I don't understand this change of attitude towards people of different faiths, particularly after the many lovely, educated and understanding conversations about religion that I had had with my daughter Madeleine's boyfriend at the time, Salim. Our understanding of religion is remarkable similar; I find the same thing with my wonderful friend Feroze Dada.

From there, we moved out of the Jewish Quarter, found a Fanta and then walked down the hill passing a large church dedicated to St Peter, thought to be the site on which he denied knowing Christ three times before the cock crowed. We entered what is now a big area called the City of David, which is currently being extensively excavated. There is a lot of politics involved here with everybody staking their claims to their history in this ancient place. From there we went further downhill and finally found The Pool of Siloam, which was not at all as I had imagined; there were hundreds of school kids there making a terrible racket, and the water looked none too clean. Having walked a long way downhill from the Old City in the serious heat, I realized that we were going to be walking back up the same hill. In this, I was wrong. We walked back via an ancient tunnel from David's time. You can wade down the tunnel through water one way, i.e. on the way down, but the way back up the tunnel is on a dry path. It wasn't the most pleasant thing I have done; we were all in a line with the myriad school kids and it was claustrophobic, but it did take us all the way back up the hill in about half an hour and brought us out close to the Western Wall. We then went further uphill to the Armenian gate, re-entering the Old City in a part I had not seen before. We found the church built on the site where the Last Supper is meant to have taken place. I am a trifle dubious about this, a bit too Crusader to be real perhaps, but does it matter? So much of Jerusalem contains so much authentic history on a grand scale.

The icon of the Last Supper (page 105) shows Jesus at the centre with the beloved disciple, John, leaning towards him. Judas is off to the left of Jesus and not part of the main group. Mary Magdalene is also present, bringing the number at table to fourteen.

Luke 22:7–23

Then came the day of Unleavened Bread on which the Passover lamb had to be sacrificed. Jesus sent Peter and John, saying, "Go and make preparations for us to eat the Passover."

"Where do you want us to prepare for it?" they asked.

He replied, "As you enter the city, a man carrying a jar of water will meet you. Follow him to the house that he enters, and say to the owner of the house, 'The Teacher asks: Where is the guest room, where I may eat the Passover with my disciples?' He will show you a large room upstairs, all furnished. Make preparations there."

They left and found things just as Jesus had told them. So they prepared the Passover.

When the hour came, Jesus and his apostles reclined at the table. And he said to them, "I have eagerly desired to eat this Passover with you before I suffer. For I tell you, I will not eat it again until it finds fulfilment in the kingdom of God."

After taking the cup, he gave thanks and said, "Take this and divide it among you. For I tell you I will not drink again from the fruit of the vine until the kingdom of God comes."

And he took bread, gave thanks and broke it, and gave it to them, saying, "This is my body given for you; do this in remembrance of me."

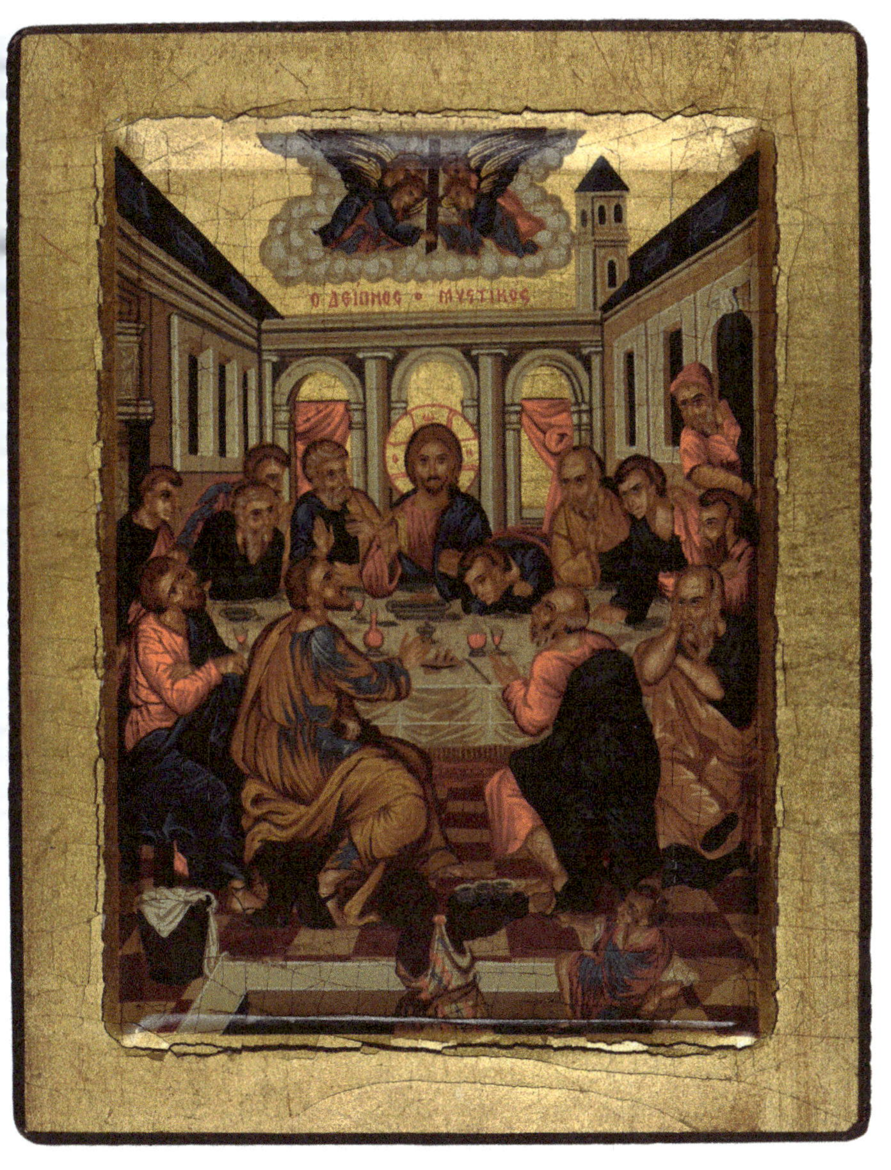

The Last Supper

> In the same way, after the supper he took the cup, saying, "This cup is the new covenant in my blood, which is poured out for you. But the hand of him who is going to betray me is with mine on the table. The Son of Man will go as it has been decreed. But woe to that man who betrays him!" They began to question among themselves which of them it might be who would do this.

From here we passed the Church of the Holy Sepulchre and scuttled back to the hotel where we had a light lunch. Thereafter, I had a sleep and then went for a swim. Andrew went to St George's Cathedral and saw the room where Allenby took the Ottoman surrender, and then was shown the courtyard where his great-uncle had been photographed.

I had investigated getting Mosa to drive us to Abu Ghosh, one of the three sites of Emmaus, where Christ met two disciples on the road; it was 300 shekels and we, therefore, decided to drive it ourselves in our hired car. Of course, we became quite lost and had great difficulty finding the Crusader Church, because in fact the door to enter the site looked locked, so I didn't recognize the site from my previous visit. Luck was with us, because although it looked locked, it wasn't, and we were able to go in. Andrew read the piece from St Luke about the road to Emmaus, which fits with our penultimate icon.

This is a very unusual iconographic theme which I have long sought. Renaissance art's most famous depiction of this theme is the famous Caravaggio painting where Christ breaks the bread and is recognized by his two walking companions, Simon and Cleopas.

Luke 24:13–18, 28–31

> Now that same day two of them were going to a village called Emmaus, about seven miles from Jerusalem. They were talking with each other about everything that had happened. As they talked and discussed these things with each other, Jesus himself came up and walked along with them; but they were kept from recognizing him.

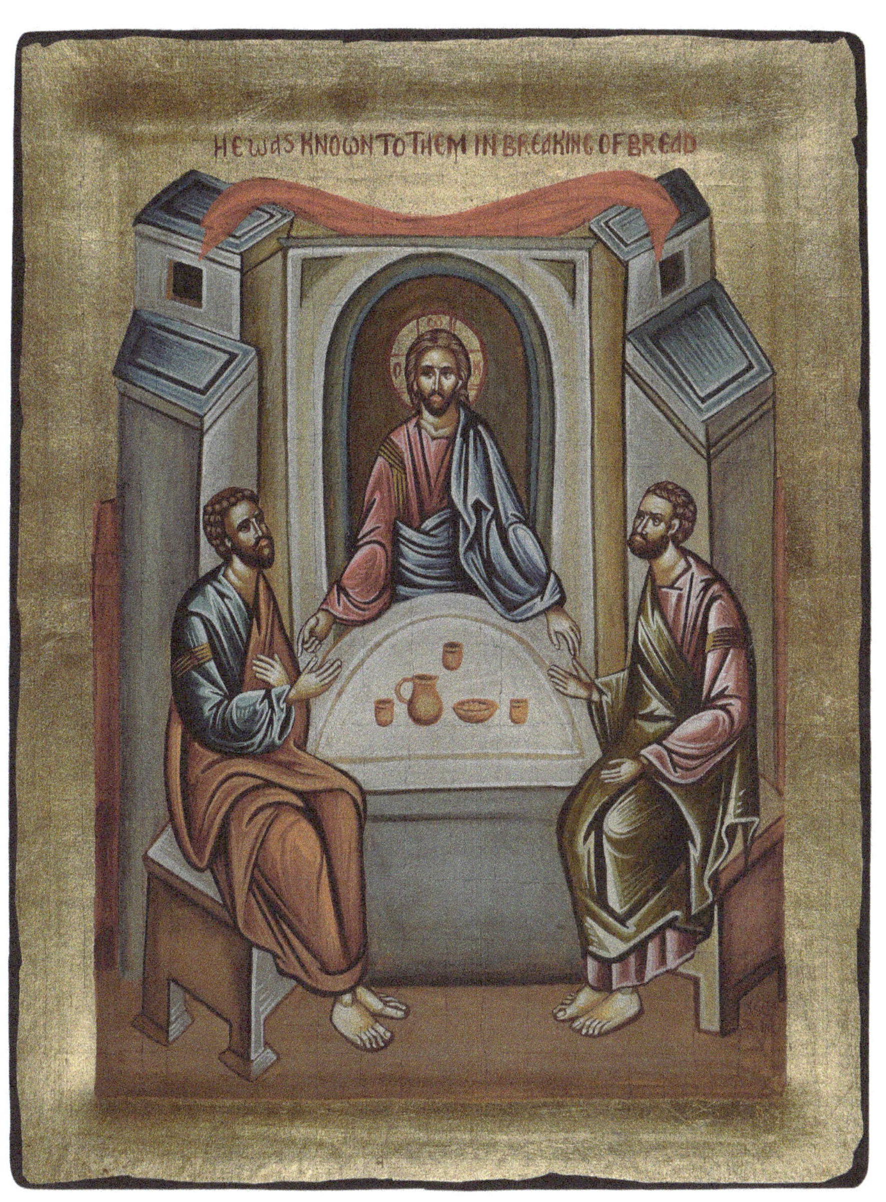

Emmaus

> He asked them, "What are you discussing together as you walk along?"
>
> They stood still, their faces downcast. One of them, named Cleopas, asked him, "Are you the only one visiting Jerusalem who does not know the things that have happened there in these days?" . . .
>
> As they approached the village to which they were going, Jesus continued on as if he were going further. But they urged him strongly, "Stay with us, for it is nearly evening; the day is almost over." So he went in to stay with them.
>
> When he was at the table with them, he took bread, gave thanks, broke it and began to give it to them. Then their eyes were opened and they recognized him, and he disappeared from their sight.

I had the great good fortune to have had this read to me by my friend, Father Gary Bradley, on my last visit. The Crusader Church was built to mark the place. When I had told Andrew the story, he asked me if I could find this iconographic theme for him. I pored over many books of icons, but the theme did not exist. Imagine my delight to be in one of the chapels of Tolleshunt Knight Monastery in Essex, and there it was. What you see on page 107 is the repainted version, done by a monk in Athens, and it is only here due to the efforts of Maria Andipa, to whom I owe a debt of gratitude. This icon ironically is now widely available; it's in St Paul's shop next to Westminster Cathedral in London. It is a clever composition borrowing from the Rublev Trinity.

St Luke, after describing the Emmaus encounter, thereafter restricts his post-resurrection writing to the following:

Luke 24:36–43

> While they were still talking about this, Jesus himself stood among them and said to them, "Peace be with you."
>
> They were startled and frightened, thinking they saw a ghost. He said to them, "Why are you troubled, and why do doubts rise

in your minds? Look at my hands and my feet. It is I myself! Touch me and see; a ghost does not have flesh and bones, as you see I have."

When he had said this, he showed them his hands and feet. And while they still did not believe it because of joy and amazement, he asked them, "Do you have anything here to eat?" They gave him a piece of broiled fish, and he took it and ate it in their presence.

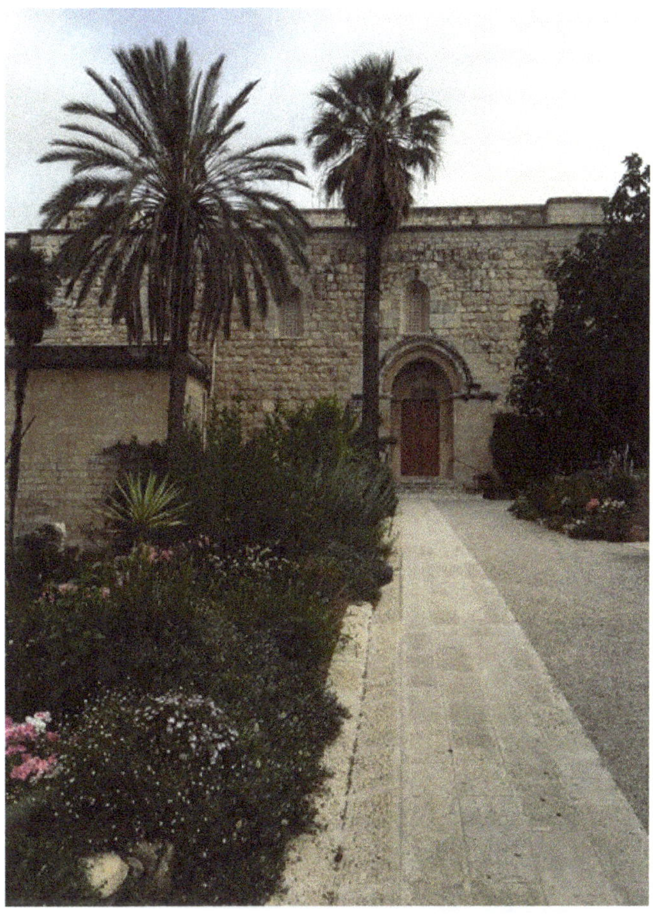

Emmaus, Church of the Resurrection, Abu Ghosh

Back in Jerusalem, I would love to say where, but it isn't known, Christ again appeared to the disciples again and on this occasion, St Thomas was present. He puts his hand in Jesus' side.

This icon (page 111) shows the risen Christ in the centre; he has the wounds of crucifixion on him and is surrounded by the disciples. St Thomas is placing his hand into the wound in Christ's side as Jesus had predicted. St Thomas has been much maligned for this lack of faith, as Doubting Thomas. As a surgeon I have to say I am all with him; if I had been there, I would have wanted to examine Jesus. There is never any harm in a bit of proof! In John's Gospel (20:24–29) Jesus has appeared to the disciples, but Thomas was not there:

> Now Thomas (also known as Didymus), one of the Twelve, was not with the disciples when Jesus came. So the other disciples told him, "We have seen the Lord!"
>
> But he said to them, "Unless I see the nail marks in his hands and put my finger where the nails were, and put my hand into his side, I will not believe."
>
> A week later his disciples were in the house again, and Thomas was with them. Though the doors were locked, Jesus came and stood among them and said, "Peace be with you!" Then he said to Thomas, "Put your finger here; see my hands. Reach out your hand and put it into my side. Stop doubting and believe."
>
> Thomas said to him, "My Lord and my God!"
>
> Then Jesus told him, "Because you have seen me, you have believed; blessed are those who have not seen and yet have believed."

I know St Thomas has helped me a great deal. The other aspect of this icon which I think is unique is that it allows one by proxy to kiss the body of Christ via St Thomas's hand. The Orthodox tradition is clear: one can kiss the hands of saints but only at most the feet of Christ. This icon makes for an exception, although I am sure this may be regarded as wrong thinking.

From Abu Ghosh, we returned to our hotel for a splendid repast of potato and roasted garlic soup followed by Wiener schnitzel for me and

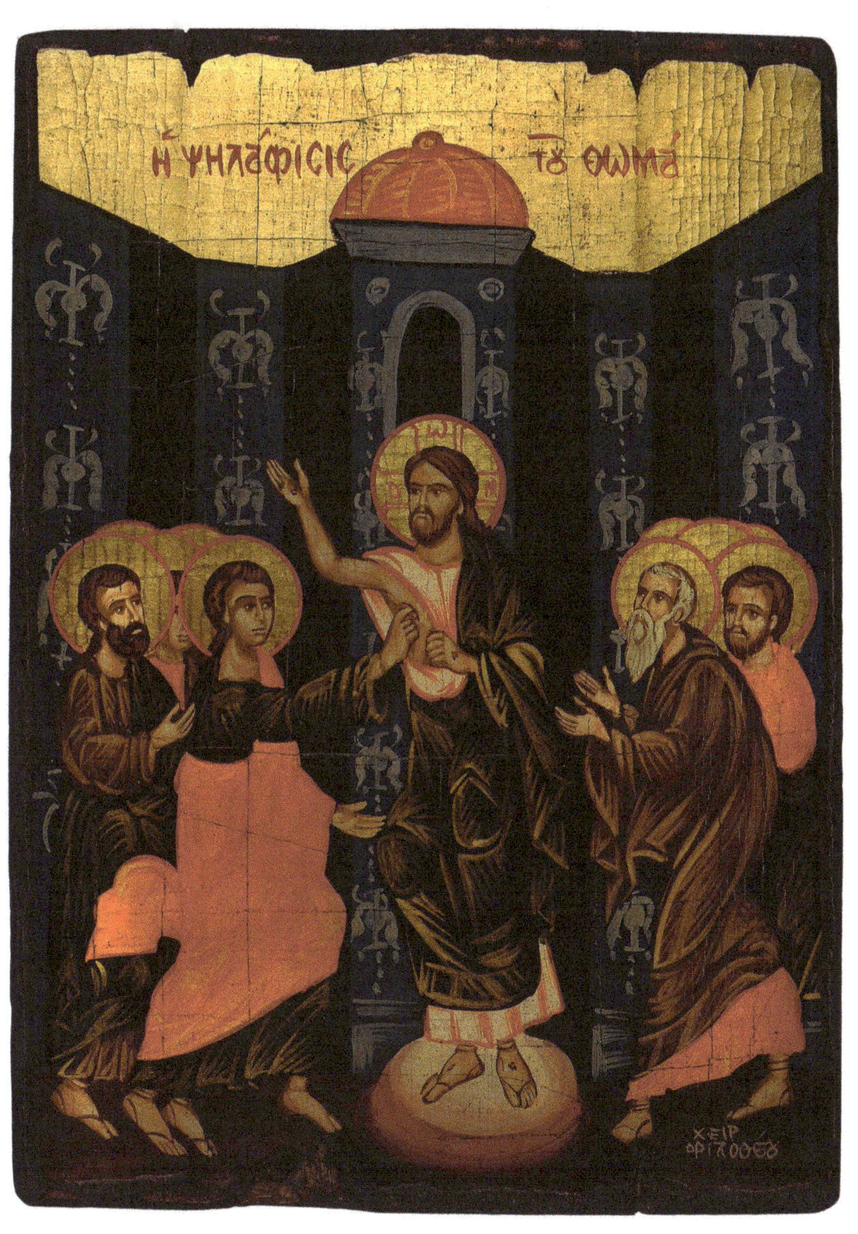

St Thomas and the Risen Christ

chicken for Andrew. The Wiener schnitzel was a bit on the large side. Then off to bed. Our last day was spent souvenir hunting and buying some presents, including multiple rosaries for Fr Gary, at the same shop we had patronized the last time I had been there with him. It was then off to the airport and home. What an amazing trip.

Final reflections

I sincerely hope, my dear reader, that the four underlying messages of this book have come through. The Veil of Manoppello, the original image, may well be the original image of Christ "not made by human hands". As such it could be regarded as the progenitor of all icons, and its greatest significance if it is as claimed, is that here is a death cloth where the person, namely Jesus, who has died, is staring out at us with eyes open. I am sorry to labour this point, but, as I said previously, so startling is it that I had to read Paul Badde's book twice before grasping this vital point! I can't help but requote St John (20:6–8) from the Authorized Version:

> Then cometh Simon Peter following him, and went into the sepulchre, and seeth the linen clothes lie,
>
> And the napkin, that was about his head, not lying with the linen clothes, but wrapped together in a place by itself.
>
> Then went in also that other disciple, which came first to the sepulchre, and he saw and believed.

I am well aware that there is much dispute around Badde's interpretation, but it is a compelling story which explains much. Come what may, we do seem to have the original icon.

If you are a person who wants to see where history was made, you can visit the sites of the events portrayed in the icons. I hope this book has succeeded in giving you at least a flavour of "then and now".

Icons themselves are not the dull art form perceived in the West but tell the really important parts of the New Testament story. They are a perfect adjunct to contemplative prayer and there is much hidden allegory which is interpretable once you know the genre. They are like little hidden doors to that pearl beyond price, namely the kingdom of God, which is of course within one. It's not the image but that which lies behind it, the invisible, which matters. In my previous book *The Journey* I explore The Prayer of the Heart in some detail along with its equivalents in other religions. The combination of repetitive prayer, pilgrimage to thin places, and these little hidden doors, namely icons, make for a powerful combination on the journey of life.

It is impossible to complete this book in the summer of 2021 without some reference to COVID-19. The greatest irony is that out of all the pain and suffering the world has experienced many positive things; a greater sense that humankind had better care for his planet before they destroy it, and a greater interest in the soul as well as the mind and body. I believe that this book is better timed now than it was two years ago, much of that delay being COVID-19 related. I for one had a narrow escape, but have been blessed not to have been badly affected, sadly unlike many of my friends, colleagues and patients.

To quote Dr Maya Spencer: "Spirituality involves the recognition of a feeling or sense of belief that there is something greater than myself, something more to be being human than sensory experience, and the greater whole of which we are part is cosmic or divine in nature . . . An opening of the heart is an essential aspect of true spirituality."*

Icons, pilgrimage and repetitive prayer are all routes to this opening of the heart. For the "final icing on the cake" if you can get out there, go exploring, go on pilgrimage, enlightening, invigorating and often great fun, please God go and do it. Carpe diem!

---

* Maya Spencer, "What is spirituality? A personal exploration", Royal College of Psychiatry, 2012.

Further reading

Paul Badde, *The True Icon* (San Francisco: Ignatius Press, 2010).

J. Richard Smith, *The Journey: Spirituality, Pilgrimage, Chant* (London: Darton, Longman and Todd, 2016).

Anna Kostova, *The Subject of Early Russian Icons* (Saint Petersburg: Iskusstvo Publishers, 1994).

Richard Temple, *Icons and the Mystical Origins of Christianity* (Oxford: Luzac Oriental Ltd, 2001).

EU GPSR Authorized Representative:

LOGOS EUROPE, 9 rue Nicolas Poussin, 17000 La Rochelle, France

contact@logoseurope.eu

www.ingramcontent.com/pod-product-compliance
Lightning Source LLC
LaVergne TN
LVHW052347100826
845147LV00012B/769

* 9 7 8 1 7 8 9 5 9 2 1 6 0 *